YORK MINSTER

Lucy Beckett & Angelo Hornak

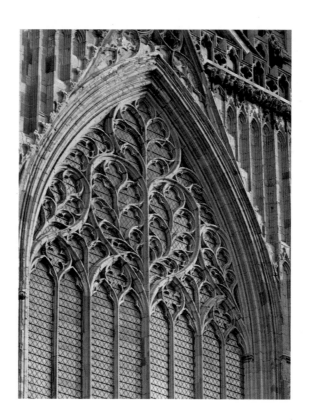

Scala/Philip Wilson

© 1981 Summerfield Press Limited and Philip Wilson Publishers Limited

First published 1981 by
Summerfield Press Limited, 6A Bedford Square, London WC1B 3RA
and
Philip Wilson Publishers Limited, Russell Chambers, Covent Garden, London WC2E 8AA.

Text: Lucy Beckett
Photographs: Angelo Hornak (except for two black and white photographs on pages 87 & 88,
which are reproduced by courtesy of Shepherd Building Group Ltd.)
Design: Paul Sharp
Edited by Philip Wilson Publishers, London
Series Editor: Michael Rose

Produced by Scala Istituto Fotografico Editoriale, Firenze
Printed in Italy

ISBN 0–85667–089–8 Pbk.
     0–85667–090–1 Hdbk.

Photographs so indicated on pages 9, 10, 43, & 69, were taken by kind permission of the
Curator, the Yorkshire Museum

The author and publishers would like to acknowledge the time and help generously given by
the clergy and staff of the Minster, the Minster Library and the Minster Stone-yard. The
author is particularly grateful for the friendly assistance of Canon Reginald Cant, Chancellor
of the Minster, whose *History of York Minster* (edited, with G. E. Aylmer, 1977) is the modern
standard work on the cathedral. The photographer would like to thank the Head Verger,
vergers and Minster police for much practical help and advice

Title page Tracery of Master Ivo's great west window,
with 'the heart of Yorkshire' at its centre, c.1330

Contents

East end of the Minster, begun in 1361, showing the elaborate pinnacles typical of the period and John Thornton's great east window completed in 1408

A Message from the Archbishop

The Minster has played a long and highly distinctive role in the life, not only of the Northern Province, but of the nation as a whole. You have only to glance at the chronology on page 5 of this book to be convinced of that: Constantine proclaimed Emperor in 306; Alcuin master of the cathedral school from 766 to 781; the Viking conquest in the ninth century and the arrival of the Normans in the eleventh; the Scottish wars from 1298 to 1337, when York was often the seat of court and government; Richard Scrope, archbishop, executed for treason in 1405; the Pilgrimage of Grace in 1536.

But the Minster is not just a monument to the past. It is the centre of a whole network of relationships — with the city of York, with the thousands who attend its great services, with the millions from this country and from overseas who pass through it every year.

The last date in the chronology is 1972: the Minster saved from collapse. Thank God that it still stands in all its glory, reminding us not only of the temporal history in which it has been involved but of the eternal truth for which it has always stood — the presence of God in His world through His Son Jesus Christ. I warmly commend this book and hope you will enjoy reading it.

Stuart Ebor:

STUART EBOR

Early fifteenth-century head high in the south transept, photographed during restoration work on the vaulting

Chronology

306	Constantine proclaimed Emperor at York
314	Early Christian bishop sent from York to the Council of Arles
625	Paulinus comes north with Princess Ethelburga of Kent
627	Baptism of King Edwin of Deira
633	Paulinus returns south
c640	Completion by King Oswald of a stone church round Edwin's baptistry, dedicated to St Peter
669–705	Wilfrid, bishop; church of St Peter restored
732–766	Egbert, first archbishop
741	Church of St Peter damaged by fire; subsequent rebuilding completed by Archbishop Aethelbert, c770
766–781	Alcuin, master of the cathedral school
866–7	Vikings conquer York
972–992	Oswald, archbishop
1061–1069	Ealdred, archbishop
1069	Church of St Peter sacked by Norman soldiers
1070–1100	Thomas of Bayeux, first Norman archbishop
1075	Last Viking raid on York; church of St Peter finally destroyed
c1080–1100	New minster built on the present site and alignment
1114–40	Thurstan, archbishop
1137	Minster damaged by fire; alterations at the east end begun by Thurstan but completed after his death
1141	William Fitzherbert elected archbishop (under royal pressure)
1147	William deposed in favour of Henry Murdac
1153	Death of Archbishop Murdac and restoration of William
1154	Death of Archbishop William (canonized 1227)
1154–81	Roger of Pont l'Evêque, archbishop; enlargement of the west end of the minster and complete reconstruction of the choir
1189–1207	Geoffrey Plantagenet, archbishop (d.1212)
1215–55	Walter de Gray, archbishop
c1220–45	Building of the south transept (as it now exists)
c1253	North transept completed by John Romanus (as it now exists)
c1260–90	Building of the chapterhouse and vestibule
1291	Building of the present nave begun
1298–1337	Scottish wars: court and government often at York
1306–16	William Greenfield, archbishop
1317–40	William Melton, archbishop
1338	Great west window glazed
1352–73	John Thoresby, archbishop
c1360	Vault of the nave completed
1361	Building of the present Lady Chapel begun
1374–88	Alexander Neville, archbishop (died in exile, 1392)
1388–96	Thomas Arundel, archbishop
c1394	Building of the present choir begun
1398–1405	Richard Scrope, archbishop (executed, 1405)
1405–8	Glazing of the great east window
1407	Partial collapse of the central tower
1407–23	Henry Bowet, archbishop
c1420	Completion of the choir (as it now exists)

View of the Minster from the north east, between the high brick walls of Chapter House Street

CHAPTER 1 *The First Thousand Years*

St Luke, from the York Gospel Book, made in Canterbury c.1000, in York since 1020. The only one of ten pre-Conquest gospel books to survive the Reformation

For a brief moment, in the year 306 A.D., the site of York Minster was the focal point of the civilized world. York was then the effective capital of Roman Britain: the Roman Emperor Constantius Chlorus had made it his base for the defence of the northern frontier of the Empire, and when he died it was in York that his army proclaimed his son Constantine the new Emperor. Almost certainly the proclamation took place at the entrance to the great columned hall of the headquarters building, on its south-west side, at a point beneath the south door of the present Minster.

Such was the importance of the command at this northernmost garrison city of the Empire that Constantine was eventually acknowledged Emperor throughout the Roman world. And only six years after greeting his cheering troops in York he declared himself converted to Christianity, with the result that the beliefs of a scattered and persecuted sect became by the end of the fourth century the official religion of the Empire. As it happens, a group of these obscure Christians already existed in York in the early years of the century: in 314 a bishop from the city was one of three British bishops who travelled to Gaul for the Council of Arles. No archaeological trace of this early community has been found, and the building in which they met is likely to have been at a safe distance from the headquarters of the legionary fortress. Nevertheless, it is tempting to wonder whether York may not have provided the first Christian Emperor with some at least of his early experience of the church.

Dedication Stone of the Temple of Serapis

Second-century Roman dedication stone of a pagan temple in York; 'Claudius Hieronymianus, commander of the VIth victorious legion, built this temple to the sacred god Serapis'. This was one of the cults which eventually gave way to Christianity

(Courtesy of the Yorkshire Museum)

Head of the Emperor Constantine, from a twice life-size statue which stood near the Roman headquarters; early fourth century

Roman tombstone of a York legionary
officer, with roses
(Courtesy of the Yorkshire Museum)

Roman tombstone of the lady Aelia Aeliana who died
in York; shown at table with her husband and
daughter
(Courtesy of the Yorkshire Museum)

Within a hundred years of the conversion of Constantine the barracks at York
were empty. The Sixth Legion was no more than a paper title for a rabble of peasants
under British chieftains, struggling to hold lines against the Picts in the north and the
Saxons in the south. The reality of Roman imperial power, the great civil and military
machine which had founded the city of York in 71 A.D., had receded from Britain for
good. As the invaders poured in and pagan Saxon kingdoms were set up where the
Romans had ruled, Christianity receded too, not only southwards to the European
mainland whence it had come, but north and west to the Celtic strongholds of Ireland
and Scotland. By the early seventh century, in northern England, only the small
kingdom of Elmet, south-west of York, retained its identity as a British and Christian
community, and in 624 even this fell to Edwin, the Saxon king of Deira. Meanwhile
in the south of England Rome had returned, no longer as a conquering army, but
more peacefully in the form of a mission from Pope Gregory the Great, bringing
Christianity to the Angles. When the light of history shines again on York, it picks out
the baptism of King Edwin in 627, in the dilapidated but still vastly impressive
Roman city which he had made his capital.

Who baptized King Edwin? Supporters of the Celtic Christian tradition put it
about later in the Middle Ages that Rhun, a priest from Galloway, had converted the
king of Deira. But the earlier and more reliable story, recorded by the great
chronicler Bede, is that St Paulinus, sent from Rome to help St Augustine at
Canterbury, came north with the Christian Kentish princess Ethelburga, who was to
marry Edwin, and a few years later baptized the king himself in a wooden church
specially built for the occasion. Paulinus is reckoned the first Bishop *of* York, the
traveller to Arles having been no more than a bishop *in* York. Pope Gregory, whose
somewhat contradictory instructions were much debated in later centuries, had
intended York to be the centre of a northern metropolitan see, the seat, that is, of an
archbishop, as London — not Canterbury — was to be in the south. Pope Honorius
sent the *pallium*, as the insignia of an archbishop, to Paulinus, but before it reached
him the darkness had descended again. In 632 Edwin was killed in battle by the
pagan king of Mercia, and Paulinus retired with Queen Ethelburga to the safety of
Kent.

Edwin's death interrupted the building of a stone church which had been designed
to surround his original wooden structure. His successor, King Oswald, finished the

stone church before his own death in battle, and this, dedicated to St Peter as the cathedral in York has been ever since, was the ancestor of the Minster we know today. It was completed in the absence of a bishop since, in the troubled north, no one succeeded Paulinus for more than thirty years, and it was almost certainly not on the site of the present Minster, where no trace of a Saxon church has been found. In the time of Edwin and Oswald, and for more than two centuries after, the great Roman fortress buildings still stood, decaying and formidable: the Saxon church may have been built a little to the north or a few hundred yards to the south-east of them.

The light of the see of York was rekindled with the appointment of a new bishop in 664, the year of the Synod of Whitby which bound together the divided Celtic and Roman Christian traditions. This time the torch certainly came from the north. The zealous and forceful Wilfrid, born in Northumbria and educated at Lindisfarne, Canterbury and Rome, was the very personification of the spirit of the Synod, in which he had played a leading part. He took so long about his consecration in France, however, that the Northumbrian king made Chad, a pupil of St Aidan and a product of the pure Celtic tradition, bishop in his absence. In 669 Wilfrid returned, Chad retired gracefully, and Wilfrid restored Edwin's neglected church, repairing the roof with lead, glazing the windows (for the first time) and whitewashing the inside. Though justly famous as a missionary and founder of churches, Wilfrid was not an easy man. He fell out several times with the Archbishop of Canterbury, setting a pattern that was constantly to recur down the ages. He acted as Bishop of York for almost forty years, until 705, but only when not at loggerheads with Canterbury, or for some other reason out of the country. Bosa, on the other hand, who alternated with him, John of Beverley who succeeded him, and Wilfrid II who succeeded John, were all three mild monks from Whitby, prepared to govern the see of York in full accord with Canterbury and Rome. So the two strains of Christianity in England did at last become one in York, the most significant single event in the process being perhaps the consecration of St Cuthbert as Bishop of Lindisfarne in the Saxon minster at York by the Greek Archbishop Theodore of Canterbury in 685.

This was the era of saints and legends. Paulinus, Edwin, Ethelburga, Oswald, Wilfrid, Chad, Bosa, John of Beverley, Wilfrid II, Cuthbert, Theodore, and Bede (from whose pen all their stories come down to us): every one of these was called a saint and venerated by later Christians. Some of them may strike us now as distinctly saintlier than others. But without their courage, orderly and settled Christianity could never have been established in those strife-torn days. And the tales about them cannot always be dismissed as fables. It was believed throughout the Middle Ages, for instance, that the head of the slain St Oswald had accompanied the body of St Cuthbert in its travels to its final resting place in Durham. Fifteenth-century folk-memory represented St Cuthbert holding Oswald's head in the centre of his window in the Minster. When St Cuthbert's tomb was opened in 1828 the king's head was there, lying on the bishop's breast.

A great period in the history of the see followed the age of saints. Egbert, a Northumbrian ordained in Rome, ruled from 732 to 766 as its first archbishop, at last receiving the *pallium* from the Pope. Bede himself had written to him with advice about how to reform the church in the north, and in York he much expanded the cathedral school and library, which now became famous throughout Christendom. He appointed as master a man whom the school's most distinguished pupil later called 'lover of justice, trumpet of law, herald of salvation'. The master was Aethelbert, who was to succeed Egbert as archbishop; the pupil was Alcuin, who became one of the greatest teachers in the history of Europe. Alcuin wrote an account in verse of the church of York, in which he listed the books in the library. They included not only the Latin fathers, Jerome, Augustine and Gregory, and more recent Latin authors like Boethius and Bede, but classical texts, Virgil, Cicero and Pliny among them, and even some Greek and Hebrew books. No other such school and library existed north of the Alps, and when Charlemagne summoned Alcuin to France to educate his household and his church, he was sending for help to a city that was once again at the centre of civilization. Alcuin's departure removed the

St. Cuthbert holding the head of St Oswald, from the St Cuthbert window, south choir transept, c.1440; the legend that the king's head rested in the bishop's coffin was already eight centuries old

intellectual leadership of Christendom from northern England to France. It was a blessing to the future of learning, nevertheless, for the darkness was gathering again over York.

Meanwhile there is news of the church of St Peter's itself in Alcuin's poem. 'The church in which Edwin was baptized' was badly damaged by fire in 741, while Egbert was archbishop. It was rebuilt in fine style, and in it Archbishop Aethelbert set up a new altar to St Paul. But Alcuin also mentions a splendid basilica with the very unusual dedication of *Alma Sophia* (gentle wisdom), which Aethelbert consecrated a few days before his death. Alcuin's account has mystified scholars. Were there now two large churches in York? If so, was the second one close to the site of the present Minster, where a Saxon burial ground, on the Roman north-west/south-east orientation, has been found? Or did Aethelbert change the site of the cathedral — for *Alma Sophia* is never heard of again, while St Peter's stays in the records? A firm answer is as yet impossible.

During Alcuin's lifetime Viking invaders destroyed the Northumbrian monastery of Lindisfarne. Seventy years later, while foreign scholars were still writing to York for the loan of books, Vikings conquered York itself. The next hundred years, from the middle of the ninth to the middle of the tenth century, are the darkest in the history of the see since the arrival of Paulinus. Archbishops succeeded each other, sometimes with gaps of several years between them, but we know little more of them than their names. The Vikings, from Denmark and later from Norway, established a flourishing commercial centre in the city. They did not wipe out Christianity or destroy the cathedral, and gradually even came round to the idea of conversion, but the school and library disappeared and the monastic tradition of the north, so closely connected with York, the tradition of Iona, Lindisfarne and Whitby, vanished in the smoke of raids from the sea. Characters like the Norwegian pirate king Eric Bloodaxe, who held court in York in the 940s, were not much interested in Pliny and St Jerome.

Part of a Saxon cross, probably tenth century; used as building material in the foundations of the Norman Minster

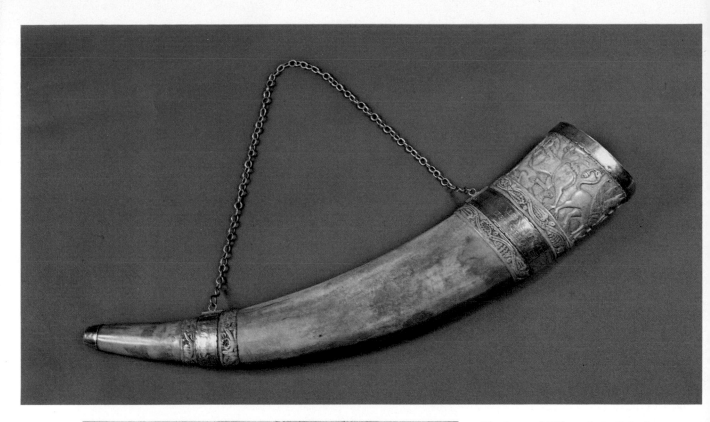

The horn of Ulf, made in Italy from an elephant tusk and presented to the Minster as token of a gift of land by an eleventh-century Viking thane

St. Matthew, from the York Gospel Book, which has been used as the cathedral oath-book since the thirteenth century

A part of Archbishop Thomas's Norman cathedral c.1080, now visible, below present ground-level, in the Undercroft; the white plaster facing is lined in red to represent ashlar

When the clouds lift again, we find something altogether new; a line of archbishops, Benedictine monks but of Danish ancestry, restoring some sort of order to the Christian life of the city and to the Minster. The most distinguished of these were the second St Oswald, archbishop from 972 to 992, and Wulfstan, archbishop from 1003 to 1023. Both were simultaneously Bishop of Worcester, and seem to have spent most of their time in their more southerly and settled diocese. The York of their day had become a largely pagan place, the most thoroughly Viking town of the whole Danelaw, and none of these monk-archbishops succeeded in restoring a single monastery to the north. But Oswald and Wulfstan were not negligible figures: when the last of their line, Archbishop Ealdred, crowned William the Conqueror king of England in Westminster Abbey on Christmas Day 1066, he came south from a cathedral to which traditional order and observance had been more or less restored.

Three years later Ealdred was dead and the metropolitan church of St Peter burned and pillaged — by William's Norman soldiers, who, though Christian, were Viking invaders themselves. Even this was not quite the end of the Saxon cathedral, which had seen so many reversals of fortune in the four and a half centuries of its existence. Thomas of Bayeux, the first Norman archbishop, collected some of the scattered clergy and patched up the building once more. But in 1075 two hundred Danish ships sailed up the Ouse, and the fighting that broke out to repel this final Viking raid 'destroyed the Minster of St Peter' for the last time.

Undaunted, Archbishop Thomas decided to abandon the old church and build a completely new one, on a true east-west orientation, and aslant the now almost flattened headquarters of the Roman legions. His masons used much Roman stone from the old fortress, facing it with hard white plaster and constructing walls seven feet thick. Archaeology has revealed the ambitious dimensions of the church they built, whose influence is still visible after 900 years: the sheer scale of its aisleless nave, massive tower and passaged choir dictated the tremendous size of the great Gothic structure that was later to rise on its deep, timber-reinforced foundations.

So the Minster we see today at last enters the story. Although scarcely a stone of Thomas's church can be seen above ground, it is still true to say of him as did Hugh the Chanter in the twelfth century: 'Ecclesiam, quae nunc est, fundavit et fecit': 'He founded and made the church that is now'. The Norman archbishop built in an almost Roman fashion, with a strong confidence and bold, plain skill, But in every sense except the material, the cathedral and metropolitan church of St Peter in York was already made when he arrived, by the real Roman, Paulinus, by the Northumbrian and Saxon saints, by Alcuin and the scholars, and by the Danish monks who brought the see of York through dreadful times.

Norman doom stone: the damned in a cauldron; devils stoke the fire. Perhaps part of an external frieze; now in the crypt

CHAPTER 2 *From Norman to Gothic*

Late Norman piers of Archbishop Roger's undercroft, decorated with chevrons and lozenges; c.1160

Damaged Norman relief of Virgin and Child, now in the crypt; c.1130

Archbishop Thomas died in the year 1100. His new church was complete, and his cathedral reorganized on an institutional pattern that survives to this day. The word 'Minster' derives from the Latin 'monasterium', but in early times this meant only a church served by a group of clergy, not necessarily monks. In York, unlike some other medieval cathedrals (Canterbury and Durham, for example), the foundation was never monastic, and the Minster was served by priests not bound by a monastic rule. Archbishop Thomas established from among this chapter of canons, as they were called, the four offices of dean, treasurer, precentor and chancellor, in whose hands the running of the cathedral lay from this time on, while the archbishops themselves became increasingly significant national figures, often away from York on the business of king or pope.

A gale of reform was now blowing through the whole of the Roman Church. The appointment by laymen, even kings and emperors, of their friends and clients to ecclesiastical high place, the buying and selling of preferment in the church, married clergy (still a recognized convention) and the consequent inheritance of offices, sleepy and luxurious living in rich monasteries — all of these were under attack. In York, where the archbishop was the most important instrument of the efforts of the Norman kings to impose order on a turbulent and still not wholly Christian population, the conflict of powerful interests produced stormy clashes in what was, after all, the century of Thomas Becket.

The career of Thurstan, archbishop from 1114 to 1140, illustrates almost every ideological collision of the age. Born in Normandy, brought up in London, a priest's son when clerical marriage was still common, he was appointed Archbishop of York by Henry I and enthroned in his cathedral before he was even ordained. Unreformed though all this was, he instantly won the lasting devotion of his chapter. He spent most of the next seven years in exile for taking a stand on the ancient rights of York as a metropolitan province equal in authority to Canterbury, the main points in his case being Paulinus's *pallium* and St Gregory's recommendation that the archbishops of York and Canterbury should alternate in seniority. He successfully but tactfully defied both Henry I and the Archbishop of Canterbury on this point (no subsequent Archbishop of York ever professed obedience to Canterbury), and returned at last to a popular welcome in York like that which fifty years later greeted Becket coming home to Canterbury. Although as a good royal servant he often travelled far from York, to London, France and Rome, on the king's affairs, Thurstan was sympathetic to the reforming spirit in the church. He looked kindly on the new monastic foundations in the north, the Augustinian canons at Nostell and Kirkham and the Cistercians at Rievaulx, and intervened — on the rebels' side — in the tremendous row at the Benedictine abbey of St Mary's, York, when the prior and twelve monks left in protest at the lax regime to form a rigorous Cistercian community at Fountains, near Ripon.

When Henry I died, leaving England to the confusion of a disputed succession, Thurstan reverted to his role of loyal lord of the north. He rallied the barons to the defence of King Stephen's realm against the Scots and inspired the victory won at the Battle of the Standard near York in 1138. He died twelve days after resigning his see to become a Cluniac monk (an old-fashioned order by then) in fulfilment of a vow made as a young man. In 1137 a bad fire, one of the omens of disaster marking Stephen's chaotic reign, had seriously damaged the Minster. The repairs, involving changes to the east end of the cathedral and extensions to the transepts, were probably set on foot by Thurstan, though not finished during his lifetime. Thurstan was one of the most attractive and distinguished of all Archbishops of

Eleventh-twelfth-century Sicilian ivory casket of Arab workmanship, probably brought back from exile by St William; now in the treasury

Detail of window in north choir aisle c.1430: St William; below, the collapse of the Ouse bridge in 1153, when the saint's prayers prevented loss of life

York. Though he died a holy death and was the friend of men like St Waldef of Kirkham and St Ailred of Rievaulx, he was never himself venerated as a saint. His successor, however, was so venerated, even though the story of his life is among the odder episodes of religious history. William Fitzherbert was a Norman nobleman, related to the Kings of Sicily (more Viking invaders) and, on the wrong side of the blanket, also to King Stephen. At Thurstan's death he held the lucrative office of treasurer at the Minster, and was conspicuous for nothing more than his easy-going friendliness. The chapter, relishing their new-found right of election, shilly-shallied over the question of Thurstan's successor until finally a majority of them succumbed to royal pressure, and perhaps a bribe from William himself, and elected William. The dissenting minority, supported by a band of righteous Cistercians eventually including even St Bernard, after six years of litigation had William deposed by a Cistercian pope and replaced by Henry Murdac, the fiercely puritan abbot of Fountains. But in 1153 William's enemies suddenly melted away: the pope, St Bernard, and Archbishop Murdac died within weeks of each other and William returned to his see amid wild enthusiasm from the people of York — so wild that the Ouse bridge collapsed under their weight. In the intervening years, after a despondent visit to his cousin Roger of Sicily, he had lived an exemplary life with the monks of Winchester. A month after his home-coming he died suddenly, poisoned, it was said, by a resentful archdeacon. Whatever the truth of his enemies' accusations of loose living and simony (the purchase of his office), his city decided for him, and against what was at the time the strongest moral force in the church. No one was hurt when the bridge fell, because, they said, of William's prayers. Miracles were soon reported from his tomb in the Minster and when, in 1227, the abbots of Fountains and Rievaulx, oddly enough his enemies' successors, enquired into these and into Archbishop William's life, their case in favour of his canonization was accepted by the pope.

Meanwhile the chapter, at William's death, lost whatever nerve they had had and rapidly elected an archbishop favoured by King Stephen, the Archbishop of Canterbury, and their own suspect archdeacon. This was Roger of Pont l'Evêque who, in the next decade, supported Henry II in his struggle with Thomas Becket, even to the tune of undergoing papal excommunication. He was ultimately regarded by many contemporaries as the real instigator of the most famous murder of the Middle Ages. The story went that at Christmas 1170 he told the king that he would never have any peace while Thomas lived; Becket in his turn had called the Archbishop of York 'Totius malitiae eius incentor': 'the inspiration of all this evil'.

Roger, no doubt, was an ambitious and worldly prelate, not much interested in preserving the church's independence from royal authority — the cause in which Becket died — and ready to exploit the old rivalry between Canterbury and York for his own ends. The see of York nevertheless prospered under his care. He particularly concerned himself with the ordinary parish clergy, lamenting, perhaps rightly, the relative wealth and privilege of the now large number of monasteries in the province. And at the Minster itself he undertook a lengthy and expensive building programme which left it at his death in 1181 one of the great Norman cathedrals of Europe.

The earlier extensions to the transepts had already made them as long as their present Gothic successors. Roger now enlarged the west end of the church by the addition of a pair of towers, close together and projecting only a little beyond the side walls of Thomas's nave. Also at the west end a large chapel, later known as St Sepulchre's, was built out at an angle to the north wall of the nave. But the eastern

Pieces of chevron ornament c.1160 and other fragments re-used beneath a pier of the south choir aisle

arm of the church was entirely rebuilt. A new choir considerably larger than Thomas's, aisled, square-ended, and with small eastern transepts, rose above a new undercroft. Its windows contained panels of vivid pictorial glass, a few of which survive, re-used, in various parts of the Minster. In the present crypt, although confused by later work and alteration, some of the piers of Roger's undercroft arcades can still be seen. The undercroft was taller than the present crypt, so that flights of steps must have led up to the choir from Thomas's nave.

By the early thirteenth century the fame of the Norman cathedral at York had spread beyond the Alps. But architectural fashion was changing. In France, still closely connected to England — Henry II ruled over more of France than the French king — the first cathedrals in the 'Gothic' style had already been built. The exiled Becket was living in Sens when its new church was finished in 1168, and seven years later the Sens architect William began to rebuild the burned down choir at Canterbury in the new manner. Thirty years later still York Minister must have seemed dark, heavy and antiquated to anyone who had seen Canterbury òr travelled in the Ile de France.

Panel of twelfth-century Norman glass from Archbishop Roger's choir re-used in nave clerestory, now in south nave aisle; St Nicholas

Lesser capitals from Archbishop Roger's choir c.1160, re-used in the eastern crypt

Archbishop de Gray's chalice, paten and ring, mid-thirteenth century; found in his tomb when it was opened during restoration in 1968. The coffin was discovered to have a unique painted wooden lid, with a portrait of the archbishop, now in the treasury

Archbishop de Gray's crozier-head, mid-thirteenth century, of gilded and jewelled walrus-ivory, found in his tomb

Roger's successor, Archbishop Geoffrey Plantagenet, may have planned the enormous project of rebuilding the Minster, but it seems unlikely that this bizarre prelate set going any actual work. An illegitimate (though the only loyal) son of Henry II, he became archbishop eight years after Roger's death, having been the unordained Bishop of Lincoln since 1175. (Becket's martyrdom may have won a battle over royal abuses in the church: it certainly had not won the war.) Geoffrey, ordained at last, was Archbishop of York until 1207 when he finally disappeared to France, but his contact with his see consisted largely in long and bitter quarrels with the chapter, punctuated only by even fiercer quarrels with his brothers Richard the Lionheart and King John. He did, however, dispatch the entire cathedral treasure of York to the far end of Europe as part of Richard's Saracen ransom. The chapter later bought it back.

Calmer times returned to the see and the Minster with the appointment of Walter de Gray as archbishop in 1215. De Gray, who had been Chancellor of England for some years, was pressed on the chapter by King John three days after he had stood at the king's elbow at Runnymede while John signed the Magna Carta. The York chapter turned him down, saying that he was illiterate — which seems a curious insult to offer such a man if there was nothing in it at all — but were forced by the pope to accept him. They did not regret it. He was archbishop for forty peaceful and prosperous years. He pulled the chapter together, brought lasting order to the administration of the church in the whole province, and, in spite of being an indispensable minister of the crown during much of Henry III's long reign, left the cathedral at York in every way in a much improved condition.

De Gray was responsible for the earliest complete parts of the Minster as we see it now: the two transepts, built in the Early English Gothic manner between 1220 and 1250. Work began on the west side of the south transept, where an aisle was probably added to the Norman building. The rest of the south transept followed; remaining

South front of Archbishop de Gray's south transept c.1240, showing elaborate arrangement of windows and arcading

Left North wall of north transept c.1250; the Five Sisters lancet window with contemporary grisaille glass; the bright panel, bottom, centre light, is late twelfth-century, re-used from the Norman choir

Right Detail of patterned grisaille glass c.1250, from Five Sisters window, north transept

asymmetries show that its west wall was at an early stage moved further west. By 1230 the south transept was well enough advanced for an altar to St William (just canonized) to be set up in the north chapel of the east aisle. The north transept was being built at almost the same time, although it is thought to have been both started and finished a few years later. The interiors of the transepts are actually very similar: both have wooden barrel vaults disguised as stone with ribs and bosses, and distinctive triforium arcades gathered under round arches. The fact that they strike the visitor as quite different is attributable to the astonishing contrast between their end walls. The south wall is, outside, an elaborate Frenchified affair with gables, arcading and lancets thick on its surface. The two tiers of doubled lancet windows under an ornate rose window high in the gable are impressive but somewhat overpowering, and may have been the personal scheme of Archbishop de Gray, who made the south transept his special concern. The end wall of the north transept is so different that it is hard to believe it was built in the same decade: the Five Sisters, five tall, even lancets, the tallest in Christendom, rise above a blind arcade to be crowned by five graduated lancets in the gable. The effect is of austerity, grace and extreme simplicity, emphasized, for the interior, by the original fine-patterned grisaille glass. John Romanus, de Gray's precentor, sub-dean and finally treasurer, is particularly associated with the north transept. Whether aesthetic judgement or economy governed his decisions, it makes him a noble memorial. He was also responsible for the great central tower built at this period, which held the Minster bells and was probably topped with a wooden spire. It is thought to have been taller and heavier than the present one, though carried on less massive piers, and it collapsed in 1407.

In 1253 Walter de Gray crowned his career as 'prince of the north' (a contemporary description) with the lavish wedding in the Minster of Alexander III of Scotland to Henry III's daughter Margaret: the archbishop's hospitality cost him four thousand marks and involved the roasting of sixty oxen and other festivities on a scale to match. Two years later he died, rich in years, honour and fortune, the dubious days of King John far in the past. His burial place is the Minster's most beautiful tomb, in the south transept, in the high, light space he and his chapter had created between the dark nave and the dark choir of the Norman cathedral.

Tomb of Archbishop de Gray
(c.1255); south transept

CHAPTER 3

The Chapterhouse

Detail of decorated canopy over chapter-house seats c.1280; the shafts are Purbeck marble, the pendants carved with naturalistic foliage and stiff-leaf

The reconstruction of the Minster that began with de Gray's transepts went on almost continuously for two hundred and fifty years. In spite of changes of style during this long period, and revisions to the crossing to accommodate first a new nave, then a new choir, and finally a new tower, the building gives a powerful impression of unity. This is perhaps due most of all to its size. The magnificently ample and consistent scale of the parts makes a whole that has none of the abrupt transitions of many English cathedrals. The chapterhouse and its vestibule, however, invisible from the inside of the church, attached to it but not a part of it, have an architectural atmosphere that is altogether different. This is in some ways an accident of date. Some of the masons who had worked on the north transept in the 1250s moved straight on to the chapterhouse in about 1260. When the chapterhouse vestibule was finished some thirty years later, a younger generation of masons moved on to the building of the new nave. Nevertheless, the chapterhouse caught the particular fashion of the three decades which saw it rise, perhaps from a virgin site, perhaps from the demolished plain rectangle of a Norman predecessor. Whereas all the rest of the interior of the Minster has a majestic grandeur, a bold, almost bald, breadth and height of massive strength, the chapterhouse and its vestibule are exotic, delicate, sophisticated and experimental, in the fanciful Decorated style of their exact date.

This contrast with the main body of the cathedral is appropriate. The chapterhouse was built not for the solemnities of the liturgy, the celebration of great feasts or the intimacy of the sung office in the cold choir on dark afternoons, but for business. This, for the rest of the Middle Ages and beyond, was the nerve centre of the richest corporation in the north of England. Here the members of the Minster chapter were not so much priests as landowners, administrators, lawyers and bureaucrats. Here they made decisions, held elections, dispensed ecclesiastical justice, received the king and lent him their secretaries, parchment and ink; here they discussed candidates for the archbishopric, drafted letters to the pope, interviewed master-masons, debated privileges, compromised, haggled and fell out. The chapterhouse of a secular cathedral was a medieval board-room, and if, by historical chance, the York chapterhouse has an air of prosperous contrivance, the chance is a happy one.

After the alarms and excursions of the twelfth century, Archbishop de Gray had stabilized the government of the cathedral in the form in which it was to remain until the great upheaval of the Reformation. Four out of five of his immediate successors as archbishop — taking the line to the end of the thirteenth century — had been residentiary canons of the cathedral, working members of the chapter, before their election. The odd one of the five, Walter Giffard (archbishop 1266–79), was, it is true, an important public figure from outside. He was Henry III's Chancellor when he was appointed to the see by the pope, and later spent two years in London as regent of England between Henry III's death and Edward I's arrival in England from France. But even Giffard paid careful attention to the government of the province of York, and on the whole, during this period, there was solidarity between the archbishop and his cathedral chapter. External rows over precedence and privilege, however, continued unabated. Durham, a suffragan see but almost an independent principality, gave frequent trouble. As for the old friction between York and Canterbury, squabbles between the metropolitans about the carrying of primatial crosses in each other's provinces were chronic throughout the Middle Ages, and for centuries Archbishops of York toiled all the way to Rome to be consecrated rather than let Canterbury perform the ceremony.

While the archbishop conducted the affairs of the diocese, the province and often

Right Chapter-house and vestibule 1260–90, from north-west, showing awkward compression of vestibule windows at the angle with the north transept, elaborate decoration of tracery and buttresses, and unique octo-pyramidal roof

Below Junction of chapter-house vestibule and north transept, inside, showing considerable architectural confusion

the kingdom, the four dignitaries of the chapter, at least in theory, got on with the day to day running of the cathedral both as a building and as an institution. The dean was the chairman of the chapter and a prelate of the church in his own right. The office was richly endowed: display and lavish hospitality were always expected at the deanery. The dean retained the right of enthroning a new archbishop and in York, alone among secular cathedrals, the dean could decide whether or not to allow the archbishop to attend chapter meetings. Second in rank to the dean was the precentor,

Fine thirteenth-century cope-chest in chapter-house vestibule; the iron scroll-work recurs on the chapter-house doors

a much less wealthy official in charge of the liturgy and ceremonial in the church, and of the selection and training of choristers and vicars-choral. Third came the chancellor, who was responsible for the intellectual life of the cathedral, for the running of its grammar school, the theological skills of its clergy and the organization of its preaching. Lastly came the treasurer, almost as richly provided for as the dean, in whose special care were the relics and plate of the Minster and the fabric of the building. The rest of the chapter consisted of the thirty-odd canons or prebendaries: a prebend was an endowment of land, usually with a church or churches on it, whose resources supported a canon of the Minster while he paid a vicar to serve the parish in question. There were thirty-six prebends of York in all, a few of which were always held by the four dignitaries.

In practice things often worked out rather differently. This was a board, one might say, permanently weighed down by a large proportion of non-executive directors. The four dignitary offices, and many of the prebends too, were among the richest benefices of the English church, ecclesiastical plums that could be, and frequently were, shaken into the laps of people who had no intention of riding the rough roads to York or getting involved with tedious problems of local government and the wages of schoolmasters and carpenters. Many prebendaries never set foot in the city. A few, in the years of heavy papal patronage, never set foot in England. A succession of learned doctors of theology were very properly appointed to the chancellorship but only a minority of them lived, even temporarily, in York. Both precentors and, particularly, treasurers were often absentees who held these profitable posts in conjunction with several others and delegated their responsibilities to clerics on the spot. Even the dean was by no means always there to run his own chapter: for most of the fourteenth century the office was held by men busily pursuing careers elsewhere, sometimes in London, sometimes even in Rome. The result was that the actual work was done by the residentiary canons, those of the dignitaries and other prebendaries who chose to live in the city and draw the extra money (from the 'common fund') due to them for doing so.

Detail of canopy over chapter-house seats c.1280; there are 237 heads in all, a few recarved in 1844–5

Details of chapter-house carving: boy with fanciful beast;
triple-faced queen; mocking grotesque figure

Ingenious wooden vault of chapter-house c.1285; the painted decoration is somewhat over-restored

We must imagine, then, perhaps six or a dozen men assembling regularly in the chapterhouse, an exalted body keeping itself very much apart from the fifty or sixty junior clergy who sang the Office and said Mass in the chantries of the Minster. More canons would probably turn up for an important meeting such as the election of an archbishop or dean. And of course there were many other occasions, convocations, synods, the sittings of church courts, when the chapterhouse would fill up with a milling crowd of clergy, some of them taking part from the gallery that runs below the windows.

If the business bored them, they had plenty to look at. The elaborate stone canopies above the stalls are carved with a rich and entertaining profusion of heads, animals and leaves. Above the handsome iron-traceried doors stood thirteen silver statues, now lost, of Christ and the apostles. The star-ribbed timber vault — a stone vault was originally planned but soon abandoned — has a suggestion of fantasy about it, confirmed by the model that has now been made of the wooden roof above it, a fabulous mathematical construction unique in its ingenuity. Those forced to hang about in the vestibule outside, as no doubt many were, had some even finer carvings to examine on the capitals and bosses of the arcading and in the stone vault. But in both chapterhouse and vestibule it must have been the windows that seemed, as they do still in spite of much obscuring restoration, the most glamorous decoration of all. The tracery, patterned and complicated, is a far cry from the plainness of the Five Sisters, so recently built. The glass, certainly a good deal easier to grasp in its original state than it is now, depicts, in the vestibule, a series of tall figures, saints and symbolic personifications, under tall canopies, their shapes fitted to the high, narrow lights. In the chapterhouse, finished a little earlier, the seven large windows were designed as a complete pictorial scheme, bands of narrative panels alternating with bands of grisaille, a new compromise between Norman colour and Early English light. The central window, facing the door, showed scenes of Christ's passion, death and resurrection. Other windows were occupied by the stories of the Virgin, St Peter, St Paul, St Katherine, and one by episodes from the histories of five different saints, including Becket. The remaining window was devoted to the life and miracles of St William of York, who was here for the first time put on an iconographical par, as it were, with the most familiar saints of the church.

It had not escaped the notice of the Minster authorities that York sorely lacked a saint. At Thurstan's Battle of the Standard, the banners of Beverley, Ripon and Durham had carried the emblems of St John, St Wilfrid and St Cuthbert, all with York connections but all buried in their own churches, with faithful pilgrims flocking to lucrative shrines. St Thomas of Canterbury, irritatingly no doubt, had recently become the most popular saint in England: St Peter, remote in time and place, however exalted, did not pack the same punch as far as medieval piety was concerned. It is no denigration of St William's unassuming virtues to say that his cult was encouraged by the chapter with at least half an eye to the main chance. His relics were translated to a new shrine in 1284; his window in the chapterhouse was probably finished at about the same time. No promotional campaign, however, could turn so complaisant a figure as William Fitzherbert into a Thomas Becket or the archdeacon Osbert into a Henry II, and devotion to York's own saint remained strictly local.

Perhaps the best view of the chapterhouse and its vestibule is to be had not from its interior, where the canons deliberated and the tenants queued to pay their rents, but from the outside, particularly from the north of the Minster. Here the octagonal timber pyramid of the roof, the elegant flying buttresses, the intricate symmetry of the windows, and the extravaganza of glass and stone in the vestibule, its tall windows awkwardly compressed at the corners, contrast with the severity of the north transept. The chapterhouse was built in the era of the intellectual friars: St Thomas Aquinas died in 1274; Duns Scotus was teaching at Oxford in the 1290s; from 1273 to 1292 the Archbishop of Canterbury was first the senior Dominican and then the senior Franciscan in England. The chapterhouse has something of the elaborate brilliance of the scholastic philosophy of its period. But when St Bonaventure, 'Doctor seraphicus', Italian, the greatest Franciscan theologian of all, was nominated to the archbishopric of York by the pope in 1265, he declined the appointment on account of the worldly glory of the office.

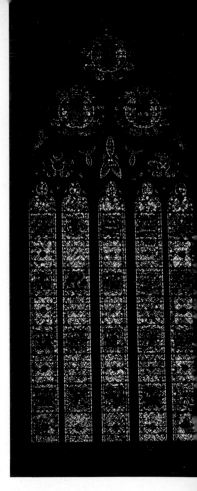

Chapter-house window c.1290, showing pattern of narrative panels alternating with grisaille; scenes from the early life of Christ, and the life of the Virgin

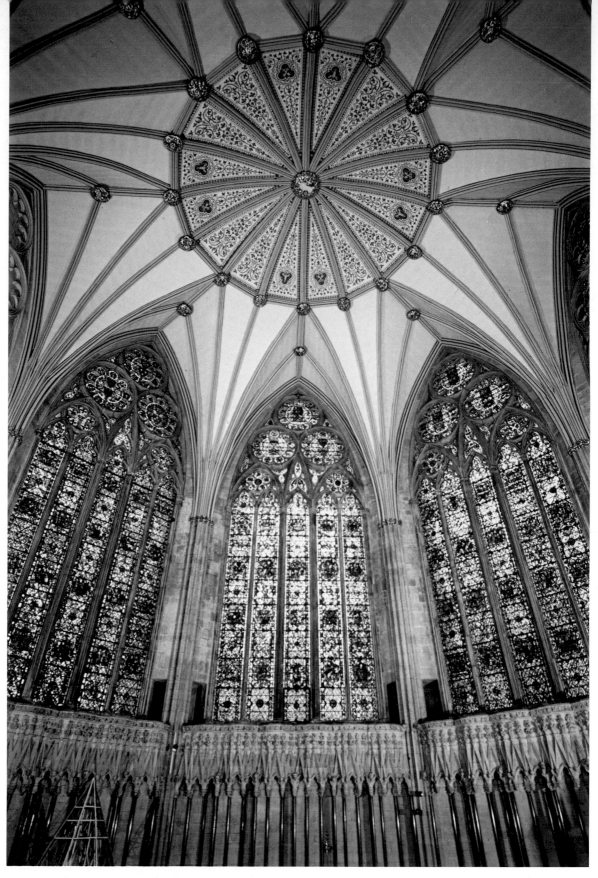

Chapter-house roof, windows and canopy. Inscribed near the door are the words: 'Ut rosa flos florum sic est domus ista domorum': 'As the rose is the flower of flowers, so is this the house of houses'

Left Finely-carved small capitals from vestibule arcading: maple-leaves and heads of medieval woodland sprites (Green Men); twining vine with leaves and grapes

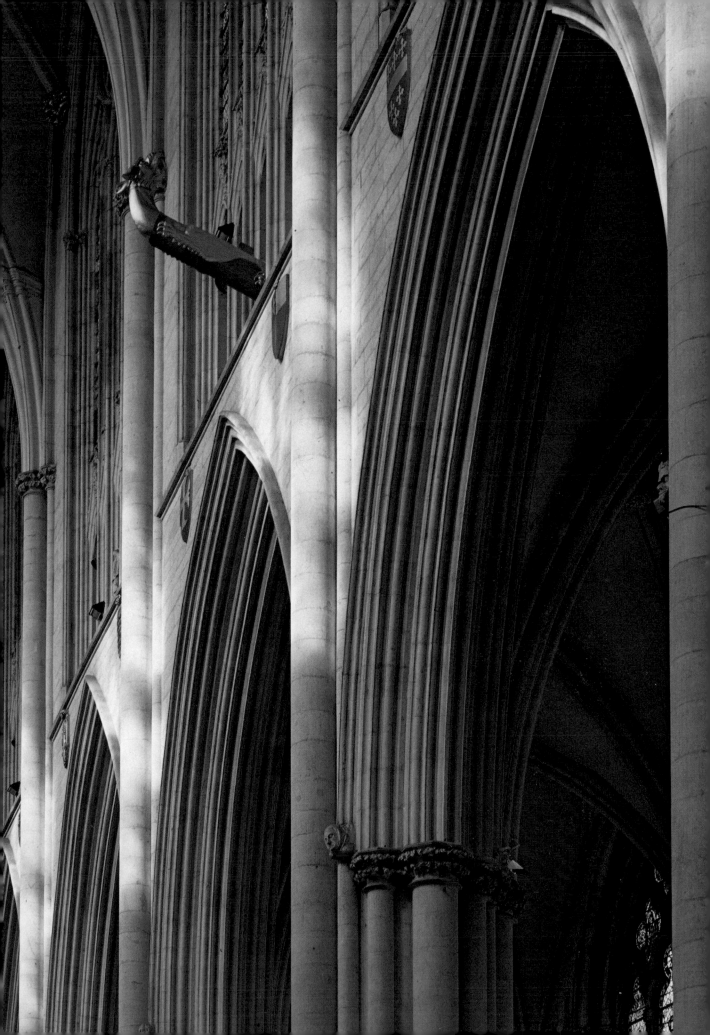

CHAPTER 4

The Nave

When the builders of the Minster, the archbishop, the chapter, and their master-masons, turned their attention in the late 1280s from the chapterhouse to the nave, they were faced with an enterprise of a very different order. Behind them — or, rather, around them as they talked — stood, just finished, a fine-wrought, up to the minute building, full of technical problems, no doubt, but on a manageable scale and separated from the daily liturgical routine of the cathedral. Down the passage and across the tranquil space of the north transept stood Archbishop Thomas's thick-walled gloomy nave, the last part of his church still intact, by now two centuries old and as solid and uncompromising as the Conquest castles built at the same time and surviving to this day. The decision to replace it with a new, aisled nave, its vault pitched even higher than the steeply gabled transepts, its vast interior lit, in the manner of the day, by huge and complicated expanses of glass and tracery, involved the Minster in seventy years of building work.

There were, of course, changes of plan along the way. Master-masons came and went; one or two of them imprinted the particular piece of building for which they were responsible with a personal style. Shifts of fashion in decorative detail can be seen here and there. But an early and fundamental decision could not be altered: the piers of the new nave were to stand on the deep, well-constructed foundations of Archbishop Thomas's seven foot thick walls. In this way the two lines of piers would run directly westwards from the great pillars of the crossing that supported the tower. The distance between them — that is, the width of the Norman church — was the guiding measurement. The new outer walls were half this distance from the piers, and each pier the same again from its neighbour. Each bay of the new side aisles was therefore square on plan and the whole structure exactly twice the width of its predecessor. The result of this simple but enormously ambitious scheme is the widest nave in England. Even though it is also, after Westminster Abbey, the tallest, it has often been judged too broad for its height. But the criterion here is the soaring vertical sweep of the French Gothic cathedrals of the Ile de France: they were of course earlier, but not, perhaps, for that reason any more 'correct'.

The nave is in any case far from being a provincial freak designed by local craftsmen oblivious of what was going on at the centre of civilization. Its second basic architectural principle, after the proportions of the ground-plan, is the elision of the two upper sections of traditional church design, the triforium or arcaded gallery running above the aisles, and the clerestory, or line of windows letting in light over the aisle roofs. For the first time in England these two elements are treated as one, the mullions of the clerestory windows running right down to the base of the triforium to form a kind of screen in front of it. This device was in full accord with the latest developments in French design: in its Geometrical suggestion of panelled surfaces, whether of stone or glass, it was also to marry happily with the English Perpendicular style of the later choir.

At first the plan seems to have been to leave Archbishop Roger's western towers where they were, at the end of the nave, although the new aisles would have projected to each side of them. In about 1320, when work had already been in progress for thirty years, it was decided to demolish the Norman towers and build an entirely new west front: exactly what the pair of western towers were intended to look like in this design it is now impossible to tell, since the front was finished only as far as the height of the nave roof, and the present top storey, parapet and pinnacles of the towers were eventually added much later. The upper part of the west front, both inside and out, does, however, differ noticeably from the style and feeling of the rest of the nave. The north and south walls, the piers and aisles and blind arcading

Arches of nave, north side, early fourteenth century. The shields bear the arms of families who fought in the Scottish wars; the wooden projection may have supported the pulley of a vanished font-cover

Nave, looking west to great west window; seventy years,
1290–1360, passed while it was under construction

Part of the elegant blind arcading which runs on the inner
surface of all three walls of the nave

Central doorway of west front; the figure holding a church
with an unfinished front is a nineteenth-century
representation of Archbishop Melton

Camel, now much battered by time and weather, on west front, mid-fourteenth century

Decayed fourteenth-century figures from west front, stored in the crypt

beneath the windows, and the three portals in the west front, have a massive strength about them, a tough grandeur in which detail is easily absorbed. Even the splendid windows of the aisles and clerestory have a masculine firmness in their Geometrical tracery. Much of this work was almost certainly directed by a master-mason known as Simon of York who died in 1322. In the early 1330s, however, a master with a highly distinctive touch had a hand in the west wall of the nave. He was probably Master Ivo de Raughton, from the Cumbrian village of that name, and the sudden burst into ogee arches (doubly curved, like two flattened Ss meeting in a point at the top) in the fourth tier of arcading both inside and outside is thought to mark his intervention in the design. The great west window, one of the chief glories of the Minster, is the work of the same master. This window, the cleverly multiplied curves and points of its tracery culminating in a heart-shaped figure, is one of the masterpieces of the English Decorated style. Perhaps the secret of the striking effect it has on the whole spectacle of the nave is the upward and outward thrust of the heart against the downward and outward pull of the window and the aisle arches. It was ready for glazing in 1338, the year in which Master Ivo disappeared from the scene. He probably also designed the

West front, finished as far as nave roof in mid-fourteenth century; the change to Ivo de Raughton's nodding ogees is visible in the fourth tier of arcading

Below Fragment, showing the eagle of St John and an angel above a nodding ogee, from the carved structure surrounding St William's tomb in nave, early fourteenth century. Archbishop Melton paid for the carving; the tomb had been empty since the translation of the relics in 1284

(Courtesy of the Yorkshire Museum)

Elaborately decorated north-west corner of west front c.1340; tower not added until the fifteenth century

elaborate base of St William's new shrine, built about this period (1320–30), only fragments of which survive. This surrounded the saint's tomb in the nave, in fact empty since the translation of the relics to a position behind the high altar in 1284.

The outer roof of the nave must have been finished by the 1330s to allow the glazing of the windows, but the vaulting caused a great deal of trouble. The aisle vaults were at first intended to be wood but ended up as stone. The planned stone vault of the nave, however, was abandoned at some stage, perhaps because of anxiety about the foundations, perhaps because of the technical difficulties of spanning almost fifty feet in stone. So in the end wood had to be used, and the present vault is a faithful copy of the original timber structure which was the last part of the nave to be finished, in about 1360. During the final twenty years or so all kinds of problems held up work on the vault. Supplies of huge oaks were hard to come by; the labourers once downed tools and stayed on strike for a lengthy period; in 1345 the master-carpenter was found to have lost his head for heights and had to be replaced by a younger man; four years later the Black Death killed the master-mason and many of the craftsmen.

South side of nave clerestory 1320–30; pinnacles and buttresses added 1905–7. Fallen fragments of masonry litter the aisle roof

Fourteenth-century timber
scissors roof of masons'
drawing-office

Medieval masons' dividers, used in drawing-office above
chapter-house vestibule

Designs of window-tracery, probably late medieval,
drawn on gypsum floor of masons' office; discarded
pieces of stonework in background

All this time, of course, the daily life of the cathedral continued while the great
space of the nave was filled with scaffolding, creaking pulleys, dust and noise, and, no
doubt, little islands of concentration where a mason, perched on a plank, chiselled a
leaf out of a band of stone or a plumber fixed a tiny pane of brilliant glass, imported
from Germany and frighteningly expensive, into a window. The masons' drawing-
office, built at this period over the chapterhouse vestibule, is perhaps the one place in
the Minster where one can recapture some sense of the careful detail of all this
protracted and complex work.

Tomb of Archbishop Greenfield (d.1316), a spirited defender of the north against the Scots; tomb built in the style of the then half-completed nave

The very large sums of money needed for the whole vast operation were raised in a variety of ways. Pilgrims to St William's shrine were now a source of profit to the Minster, though they never came in anything like the numbers that flocked to Canterbury. Indulgences were sometimes declared for those who contributed to the holy work of building the nave. Above all, successive archbishops gave moral and financial support without which the completion of the enterprise would have been impossible, and the nobility of the north joined in with substantial help both in money and in kind. The Vavasours, for instance, gave the stone for the nave from their quarries near Tadcaster, and the Percys gave timber from Topcliffe.

During the period that saw the building of the nave, York was often once more the most important city of the realm. These were the decades of the Scottish wars, the long and bloody series of campaigns in which the advantage went first one way, then the other. To fight the Scots and rule the country at the same time, Edward I, Edward II and Edward III moved court and government to York. Parliamentary business was first done from the chapterhouse in 1295, and from 1298 to 1337 the administrative machinery of the realm, clerks, secretaries, seals, treasure, tallies, and trunk-loads of documents were frequently trundled lock, stock and barrel from London. The archbishops were more than ever key figures in government, top civil servants one might say, the power derived from their authority over the province increasing their usefulness to the king — and to everyone else when the king was ineffective, as Edward II mostly was.

William Greenfield (archbishop 1306–16), an Oxford-educated protégé of Archbishop Giffard's, was a doctor of civil and canon law, counsellor and ambassador of Edward I, and finally Chancellor of England before he was archbishop. He received Edward II in York after the king's flight from his defeat at Bannockburn and, in the

Alabaster effigy of Prince William of Hatfield (d.1346); his was the only royal tomb in the Minster, where his parents, Edward III and Philippa of Hainault, were married in 1328

last years of his life, personally organized the campaign against Robert Bruce. His successor, William Melton (archbishop 1317–40) was, by contrast, a mere franklin's son from the East Riding. But he worked his way to power in the royal household, was loyal to Edward II through a good deal of thick and thin, and after the conspiracy which removed Edward II from the throne, also served Edward III as Treasurer of England and temporary Chancellor. He led forces raised by the church in the north against the Scots during one of Edward II's stickier patches and was resoundingly defeated. (The battle, at Myton-on-Swale, was scornfully christened 'the Chapter of Myton' by the Scots, 'for there slain so many priesties were'.) Melton, all the same, was perhaps the toughest, most resourceful and most lavish archbishop of the fourteenth century, and energetically encouraged the completion of the nave. He gave seven hundred pounds — then a huge sum — towards the building programme, as well as a hundred marks for the great west window and twenty pounds for St William's tomb. In 1328, at one of the grandest occasions of the Middle Ages, he married Edward III to Philippa of Hainault in the Minster, in the presence of the entire nobility of England.

With York in effect the capital of the country during these years and the knightly virtues of valour and munificence at a premium in the defence of the realm, it is hardly surprising that the Minster nave has a strongly chivalric atmosphere. Shields high on the walls proclaim the heroism of northern families in battles against the Scots and their generosity in support of the cathedral. The wonderful glass, almost all of it original, is full of heraldry (particularly in the clerestory windows), and there are portraits and coats of arms of donors, and figures of knights and merchants, scattered among the stories of the saints in the nave window. In Archbishop Melton's great west window the two rows of standing figures, archbishops on the first level and

Detail from fourteenth-century window in south wall of nave: St Peter, patron saint of the Minster, crucified upside down. The effect of this panel is enhanced by its proximity to the crucified Christ of the south window in the west wall: see next plate

Window at west end of south nave aisle 1338: crucified Christ with Roman soldiers; panels to left and right show the Virgin and St John; the donor, Thomas de Beneston, badly restored, in bottom panel

apostles on the second, are clearer and more striking than the scenes from the life of Christ on the third, and their size contributes to the overall impression of human glory which the nave conveys. Not that this is inappropriate: the nave was never intended as more than the great antechamber to the choir, which was the devotional heart of any medieval cathedral. For hundreds of years it has buzzed with pilgrims and idlers, as it does now, and was never a place primarily designed for prayer. But the two windows at the west end of the aisles strike a different note. In the north window a gentle Virgin suckles the infant Jesus; in the south window angels and Roman soldiers guard the Crucifixion. Each is plainly visible from the far east end of the Minster, more than 150 yards away, and both are full of warmth and feeling. They may serve to remind us, perhaps, that while the Scottish wars were raging and kings and archbishops were scouring the north for troops and money, the great English mystics, Rolle, Hilton and the anonymous author of *The Cloud of Unknowing*, were writing their luminous treatises on the contemplative life, also in the province of York.

Detail from fourteenth-century window in north wall of nave: a noble donor presents a window to the Minster; the arms in the borders are those of the families of Mowbray and Clare

CHAPTER 5

The Eastern Arm

South choir transept, late fourteenth century, piercing choir aisle and soaring to full height of choir roof; St Cuthbert window glazed c.1440

Perhaps since de Gray embarked on his new transepts in 1220, certainly since the beginning of the new nave in 1290, the intention of successive archbishops, deans and chapters had always been to replace the whole of the Norman cathedral with a higher, larger, lighter and more modern building. When Archbishop Thoresby in 1361 laid the first stone of the new eastern arm, he was taking his part in a continuous process that had already been going on for almost a century and a half. The Zouche chapel (in memory of Thoresby's predecessor) and the vestries beside it had already been started on foundations which were to clear the south wall of the new choir, and the masons and carpenters who had just, at last, completed the nave, now simply moved their equipment eastwards.

They began with the Lady Chapel, the four easternmost bays of the present Minster. This was started on fresh ground, outside the north and south walls of the Norman choir, with its end wall a good sixty feet further east than Archbishop Roger's east front. It could be built to its full height, therefore, and the easternmost part of it even roofed, before the old choir and the daily liturgical round conducted within it needed to be disturbed at all. The design is soberly Perpendicular, a moderate version of the English style newly developed in the south. With its massive proportions, the unadventurous tracery of its aisle windows, and the unified design of triforium and clerestory, it sustains with remarkable consistency the spirit of the nave. The only new-fangled note is struck by the dashing external screenwork of the clerestory which, against the more exuberant tracery of the clerestory windows, produces one of the most exciting architectural effects of the building. Its designer was Robert de Patrington, a master-mason from the East Riding.

Lady Chapel clerestory, late fourteenth century, showing handsome external screen and pinnacles

Minster from south. The eastern arm, from right, consists of: late fourteenth
century Lady Chapel; south choir transept; early fifteenth-century choir with
fourteenth-century vestries and Zouche chapel below

Right Elaborate gable and
pinnacles of the east end, late
fourteenth- early fifteenth-
centuries

Far right Three fine gargoyles
on south-east corner of the
Minster, at the height of the
choir roof.

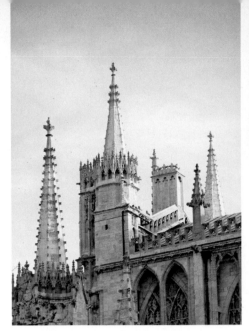

Left Lady Chapel and great
east window; the external
screen is visible through the
clerestory windows; triforium
passage immediately below

Archbishop Thoresby probably saw the completion of the Lady Chapel, except
for the great east window, before his death in 1373. A responsible and devoted
archbishop, of a type that York had fortunately been familiar with ever since Walter
de Gray, he contributed two hundred pounds a year to the building programme from
1360 to his death, and showed his concern for the ordinary priests and people in his
charge by organizing the writing and distribution of a commentary in English on the
Lord's Prayer, Creed and Ten Commandments. At a time when parsons often knew
little Latin and their congregations almost always none, this was sound, practical
pastoral care. He also finally mended the ancient feud between Canterbury and
York. Each archbishop was, at last, to be allowed to bear his cross in the other's
province; and, whereas Canterbury was to be called 'Primate of All England', York
was to have the title 'Primate of England'. That there was an element of concession in
this settlement was soon to become clear.

Thoresby was the last of a line. With the Scottish wars over, the French wars going
badly, and the now decrepit Edward III succeeded in 1377 by his ten-year-old
grandson Richard II, the brave nobility of the previous decades degenerated rapidly
into over-mighty subjects engaged in bloody factional strife. Where patient clerics
after years of labour in the royal administration had been rewarded with high office
as Archbishops of York, the job, and all the authority and wealth that went with it,
was now given to aristocratic younger sons as successive kings attempted to keep
their families' loyalty. Where archbishops' names had been those of the villages
where they were born, they were now Neville, Arundel, Scrope, the names of the
feudal clans that made and broke kings. Where Thoresby had pulled down his manor
at Sherburn to supply stone for the Lady Chapel, his successor, Alexander Neville,
quarrelled with his chapter, the city of York and most of the higher clergy in the
northern province, and sulked in his castle at Cawood while all building at the
Minster came to a halt for twelve years. Neville, a scheming protector of Richard II's
disastrous favourites, was condemned as a traitor by his rivals, outlawed and
deprived of his see, and died as an exile in Flanders in 1392. Meanwhile the
residentiary canons trying to run the cathedral cannot have been much helped by
their deans, from 1342 to 1385 three successive Roman cardinals who never set foot
in York.

The deposed Neville was replaced by Thomas Arundel (archbishop 1388–96).
Although deeply embroiled himself in the conspiratorial manoeuvring that closed
round Richard II, pushing him at last to his hysterical fall, Arundel restored relations
with the chapter and restarted the building programme. The cathedral as he found it
on his first archiepiscopal visitation (perhaps also his first visit: he was a southerner
and had been Bishop of Ely) must have been a peculiar spectacle: the vast bulk of the

nave, transepts and tower was now separated from the high walls and boarded-up
east window of the Lady Chapel by the old, dark choir. Demolition of this last
Norman part of the building began in the early 1390s; celebration of the liturgy was
transferred for the time being to the new vestry, and the construction of the new choir
was under way by 1395 and continued into the 1420s. The design was close to that of
the Lady Chapel but not identical with it: in particular the tracery and screen of the
clerestory were now reversed, the tracery being on the outside wall and the screen,
across an internal passage, on the inside wall. The result is that the four western bays
of the choir give a somewhat jerky impression when compared to the flowing lines of
the Lady Chapel. But between the two comes an architectural oddity that is also a
triumph: an eastern transept which is not really a transept since it does not project
outside the choir walls, but breaks into the aisle vaults on each side, north and south,
soaring with an immensely tall window the full height of the choir roof. The
clerestory passage continues across these windows, carried on the aisle arcade and
making an elegant bridge from the choir to the bays of the Lady Chapel.

Pier in south choir aisle; the stained-glass reflections on the creamy magnesian limestone are from the St Cuthbert window

Narrative window in south choir aisle c.1410, showing scenes from the life of the Holy Family. Probably the work of John Thornton

During the decades that saw the building of the choir, the ugly drama surrounding the throne of England produced violent repercussions in the see of York. Richard II had close ties with Archbishop Arundel. The king gave money for the work at the Minster and came to inspect its progress. In 1396 he translated Arundel to Canterbury: the archbishop's acceptance of this promotion, the first such move in the eight centuries since Paulinus, indicates the ground lost to Canterbury by Thoresby's settlement. While Arundel at Canterbury became one of the king's bitterest enemies and was banished (to return, after Richard's murder, to crown the triumphant Henry IV), York received an Austin friar for its archbishop — but only as a piece of news, since Robert Waldby never came to York in the two years left before his death. The chapter, perhaps hoping to exert a little authority for a change, elected a sound Yorkshire cleric, Bishop Skirlaw of Durham, as Waldby's successor in 1398 but were immediately over-ruled by the now desperate Richard II, who installed another aristocratic friend, Richard Scrope.

Scrope, related to half the nobility in the north, was perhaps the most romantic

Tomb of Archbishop Scrope (executed 1405) in north-east corner of Lady Chapel, with the Scrope arms in stages of heraldic complication; for many years the object of popular devotion in spite of Lancastrian disapproval

Page from Bolton Hours, early fifteenth century, in which Archbishop Scrope is represented as a saint: 'St Richard Scrope pray for us', says the suppliant lady

and also the most tragic figure of all the ninety-four bishops and archbishops who have ruled the see of York. A brave, generous, learned and virtuous man, he nevertheless betrayed two kings and died a traitor's death. Only a year after Richard II had personally secured him the archbishopric, he stood in the Tower of London with other lords to hear the king's pathetic statement of abdication, and himself read it out to parliament. Apparently a loyal servant of Henry IV, in 1405 he joined his kinsmen the disaffected Percys in revolt against the new king and, in full armour, led several thousand men in a Yorkshire rebellion. He was tricked into surrender and condemned by a summary court of peers while the king breakfasted with Archbishop Arundel of Canterbury in another room of Scrope's own house at Bishopthorpe. He was executed under the walls of York amid a huge crowd on the feast of St William. All this, of course, was the stuff of martyrdom and sainthood. Henry IV, somewhat lackadaisically, allowed his body to be buried in the Minster, under coats of arms recording the munificence of generations of Percys and Scropes, and within three months popular pilgrimage to the miracle-working shrine of 'St Richard' in the far north-east corner of the Lady Chapel was established as a tradition that was to survive for a hundred years. Henry IV was lucky to escape excommunication for himself and official canonization for his archbishop, and Henry V ten years later still suffered from sufficient vicarious guilt to found the monasteries of Sheen and Sion as Shakespeare's

'Two chantries where the sad and solemn priests
Sing still for Richard's soul.'

Scrope, in any case, was a man of obvious quality, quality possibly great enough for one to say that if he thought Richard II too far gone in folly to reign and Henry IV a tyrannical usurper, he may have been right.

John Thornton's great east window 1405–8. This window, the size of a tennis court and supported by a fine internal screen, is the largest area of medieval painted glass in the world

After this catastrophe the see was vacant for two and a half years. During this time Bishop Skirlaw re-enters the story, possibly hoping to be re-elected to the office from which he had been ousted by Richard II's appointment of Scrope. His hopes, if they existed, came to nothing: he died in 1406 while the matter was still unresolved. But in the meantime he had made a gift to the Minster which ensured him an immortality many archbishops might have envied. In 1405 he commissioned and paid for the glazing of the east window of the Lady Chapel. The master-glazier was John Thornton of Coventry, who finished the window, no doubt with considerable studio help, in three years. This window is not only the largest expanse of medieval glass to

Top row of narrative panels from great east window 1405–8; from left; the second to fifthin deys of creation; Adam and Eve and the Tree of Knowledge; the expulsion from Eden

survive anywhere: it is a masterpiece of narrative design, comparable to some of the great Italian fresco cycles. It tells the story of God as alpha and omega (who appears in the central light at the very top), of those who praise him (angels, patriarchs, prophets and saints in the tracery lights), of the beginning of the world (the book of Genesis and the story of Israel to the death of Absalom, in twenty-seven scenes), and the end (the Apocalypse, in eighty-one scenes). For all the troubles of the disturbed years in which it was made, the window is a serene celebration of God and his creation which adds to ancient belief a fresh delight in the natural order and in the infinitely varied individual men who inhabit both heaven and earth. The glass-painting has a sunny glory like that of the poetry of Chaucer, who died five years before the window was begun. At the centre of the bottom row of panels, which show legendary and historical figures from York's past, Skirlaw kneels, deserving, the spectator may well feel, his honourable place.

Bottom central panel of great east window: the donor, Bishop Skirlaw of Durham (d.1406), kneeling at his altar

Relics of the political history of the times are scattered about the eastern end: heraldic pride, and sometimes defiance, in family coats of arms; martyrdom scenes to point parallels, and the juxtaposition of Scrope and St William to establish the new saint against royal disapproval; Scrope's own tomb, upon which no effigy was allowed; the tomb of Prince William of Hatfield, the second son of Edward III, who might, had he lived, have become the good uncle Richard II so badly needed; most poignant of all, the chained white hart high on a pillar, the oddly appropriate emblem of the trapped king himself, carved when he contributed to the building of the choir. But the great east window dominates, as it should, the whole choir and Lady Chapel and restores once more, as no doubt it did when it was first made, the sense of the cathedral's primary and eternal purpose.

Chained white hart, the badge of Richard II, high on south-east pier of crossing, carved c.1390 when the king gave money for the rebuilding of the choir.

Zouche chapel, early fourteenth century; cupboards where the Minster's treasure was kept for centuries

Well and sink in south-west corner of Zouche chapel; the water supply is from a still functioning Roman well; the carved stone arch is probably Tudor, the sink Victorian

Miscellaneous quarries of medieval glass, showing that glass-painters had their lighter moments; once probably invisible in large windows, now in the Zouche chapel at eye-level

CHAPTER 6

The End of the Middle Ages

In 1407, while work on the windows and vaulting of the eastern arm was still in progress, part of the central tower of the Minster collapsed. 'A horrible tempest' was blamed, but current alterations to the crossing may have weakened the tower's support. Its four great piers were still (as they are to this day) the central piers of Archbishop Thomas's cathedral of the 1080s, although much enlarged by a casing of later masonry. Henry IV, by now no doubt thoroughly embarrassed by the goings on at Archbishop Scrope's tomb, dispatched to York not only the master-mason of Westminster Abbey to solve the architectural problem, but also a new archbishop. The mason, Master William Colchester, supervised the completion of the eastern arm and the strengthening of the crossing: the two screen arches inserted at the entrances to the choir aisles (with a sliding joint against the piers which actually allowed them to move while adjusting to their load) are his work, and he may also have planned the exceptionally solid choir screen, which was not built until later. He designed a new central tower, not begun until after his death in 1420, and never completed according to his intentions.

The new archbishop, Henry Bowet, was the first choice of neither king nor chapter. Immediately after Scrope's execution they had elected Thomas Langley, then dean of York, who later became Chancellor of England and a cardinal; but the pope, disgusted with both Henry IV and the see of York, sent him to Durham instead. Bowet, a less distinguished man, had been banished by Richard II for his desertion to Henry IV. He devoted the rest of his life — he died in 1423 — to the northern

Right Screen arch with sliding joint at entrance to south choir aisle; inserted c.1415 to strengthen the south-east crossing pier

Left View through parapet opening of central tower, built 1420–30, after the collapse of the thirteenth-century tower

Damaged but still handsome canopy over the tomb of Archbishop Bowet (d.1423) in the Lady Chapel

province, even, as an old man, setting out with the army to defend England against the Scots while Henry v was besieging French towns. With his financial help, the work on the choir windows continued and a new cathedral library was built, at an angle to the south transept, to house a collection of books left by his treasurer: this was the first library worthy of the name that the Minster had seen since the Viking invasions. Cardinal Langley survived him by fourteen years and, like Skirlaw before him, did not forget York. His executors paid for the great St Cuthbert window of the south choir transept, to match the St William window given by Lady de Ros of Helmsley on the north side of the choir.

Meanwhile Henry v had died in 1422, leaving the morally shaky Lancastrian throne and the protracted decline of the French wars into English defeat to his nine-month-old son Henry vi. The long minority, and then the unworldly mildness and mental frailty of the beleaguered king, gave his ambitious uncles and cousins their fatal opportunity. The struggle for power which began in the 1420s and culminated in the slaughter of the Wars of the Roses was not over for more than a hundred years. With the realm torn apart by bitter political rivalries, episcopal civil servants were less concerned with their sees than with stabilizing the throne and keeping some sort of government in being. Cardinal Kemp, Archbishop of York from 1426 to 1452 and Chancellor of England for much of that time, spent a fortnight in his province three times in twenty-six years. On him depended, at

Western towers, completed from height of nave roof by c.1460; their developed perpendicular panelling and crocketed pinnacles contrast with the plainness of the north transept, left. The north-west tower, right, has been the Minster belfry since its completion

Central tower, completed,
without the intended second
stage, by c.1430

repeated moments of crisis, the security of the kingdom. But he was disliked by the
chapter and unpopular with the people of the north, and he contributed nothing to
the life of his cathedral. He died as Archbishop of Canterbury in 1454, just before the
final outbreak of civil war. Two of his three successors at York, the half-brothers
William and Lawrence Booth (archbishops 1452–64 and 1476–80) were tenacious
ecclesiastics of the same stamp who veered successfully between York and Lancaster
according to the prevailing political wind. Between the Booths, York had an
archbishop who dragged the city and the Minster into the very eye of the storm.

The career of George Neville illustrates the absolute subordination of the church
to politics in the middle of the fifteenth century. Brother of Richard Earl of Warwick,
known as the Kingmaker, and first cousin of Edward IV, at fourteen he was
prebendary of Masham (the richest prebend in the Minster), at twenty-seven Bishop
of Exeter and Chancellor of England, and at thirty-two Archbishop of York. His
enthronement in 1465 was a magnificent occasion fraught with the tensions of
sinister dynastic drama. The Neville family, now the mightiest in the land, appeared
in force, parading their Yorkist allegiance. At the feast afterwards the chief guest was
the new king's brother, the Duke of Gloucester, eighteen years later and by murky
paths to become Richard III. Lower down the table sat Anne Neville, aged ten, the

Vault of central tower c.1470; the central boss, five feet across, shows St Paul with Epistles and sword, and St Peter with church and keys; the four large corner bosses show the angel, lion, bull and eagle of the Evangelists

archbishop's niece, who was to marry Henry VI's doomed son and later the Duke of Gloucester himself, and her elder sister Isabel who was to marry 'false, fleeting, perjur'd Clarence', another brother of Edward IV also present at the feast. Edward IV himself stayed away: the host, Warwick the Kingmaker, did not like the Queen (and was soon to murder several of her relations).

The Minster where this demonstration of power took place was, at last, almost complete. In spite of neglectful archbishops, the building programme of two-and-a-half patient centuries was slowly reaching its close. Master Colchester's plan to rebuild the central tower with the bells in its second stage, above the lantern, had been abandoned, probably because of concern about the weight which the piers and foundations would have to carry. Instead, the north-western tower had been designated the new belfry and the central tower was raised only to the battlemented top of the lantern. By 1465 all three towers were probably almost finished in their present form and presented, as they do today, a characteristic and striking uniformity of height. The choir screen, designed in Henry V's reign to accommodate statues of all the Kings of England since William I, had been built under Henry VI with an extra niche and statue added at the right hand end. Perhaps not everyone at that lordly gathering of the Neville connection in 1465 was unaware of a painful irony: looking

Fine late perpendicular carving; fragment from the last and grandest shrine of St William, built c.1470 for the rededication of the completed Minster; broken up in 1541 to please Henry VIII

(Courtesy of the Yorkshire Museum)

Left Choir screen, completed c.1460, with the eighth niche, right, added for Henry VI; his statue is a replacement of 1810: the original was removed by Yorkists after his death

Below Silhouette of Minster as finally completed, from north; from left, pinnacles of east front; chapter-house roof; central tower; western towers. The separate lancet-windowed building in front of the north transept is the thirteenth-century arch-bishops' chapel, restored as the Minster Library in 1810

down on the procession as it passed the screen was the most recent piece of work in the cathedral, the stone figure of the poor deposed king who still had six years to live. During that time the Nevilles turned against Edward IV — the archbishop even holding him prisoner for a while — briefly restored Henry VI, and then came to grief at Edward's hands. By 1472, when the dean and chapter decided that the Minster was at last complete and held a great re-dedication ceremony to mark the occasion, Henry VI had been murdered, Warwick the Kingmaker killed in battle, and the Archbishop of York banished to France. The Nevilles had changed sides once too often.

The completed interior, looking east; the stone, cleaned 1972, glows with white and coloured light from the windows. The present organ has been rebuilt several times since the fire of 1829

Memorial window, now in west wall of north transept, to Sir Richard Yorke (d.1498), twice Lord Mayor of the city and a supporter of Richard III. Panels, originally in the church of St John, Ouse-bridge, include a rare representation of the Trinity, and portraits of Yorke (kneeling alone), his six sons (in blue), his wife and three daughters

The stability achieved by the last forceful decade of Edward IV's reign did not endure. At his death in 1483, his brother Gloucester had the two little princes declared bastards and (almost certainly) murdered in the Tower, while he himself became King Richard III. The new Archbishop of York, Thomas Rotherham, a protégé of the little princes' mother, did his best to defend their claim to the throne and was deprived of the Chancellorship of England for his pains. When Richard, the last achievement of the Nevilles, came in triumph to the Minster after his coronation and had his son made Prince of Wales in the city, the Archbishop of York was not present.

Curiously enough, considering his subsequent reputation, Richard III was, of all the medieval kings of England, the only one who inspired deep personal loyalty in York. He was a familiar figure in the city and in the cathedral, brought up in the north, and its ruler for eleven years under his brother; his Council of the North was a successful administrative machine (later revived, to their profit, by the Tudors). Yorkshire people remembered him for generations with an affection that gave his considerable virtues their due and disregarded his crimes. His son died in 1484 — perhaps fortunately, since unwanted heirs to the throne were noticeably expendable in those violent times — and he himself, of course, in 1485 on Bosworth Field was 'piteously slain and murdered to the great heaviness of this city', as the York record put it. He fought the Tudor usurper in the company of faithful Scropes, Vavasours and Percys, while Archbishop Rotherham lived another fifteen years to become a reliable servant of Henry VII.

In 1485 there was no reason to believe that the troubles of the realm were over. To the northern province, with its love for Richard III and its traditional Yorkist sympathies, Tudor law and order, backed by a remarkably weak title to the throne, appealed less than they did in the south. Absentee archbishops did nothing to bind the north to the new dynasty. Archbishop Savage (1501–7), an old Lancastrian, insulted the chapter and the see by sending a deputy up from London to be enthroned in his place. Archbishop Bainbridge (1508–14) disappeared to Rome in 1509 as Henry VIII's ambassador, became a plotting Renaissance cardinal and never returned to England. As for Archbishop Wolsey, the very unfamiliarity of the title is some indication of how little attention the great Cardinal paid to his province in the north. Busy in London amassing the tremendous personal power which both illustrated all the abuses known to the medieval church and at the same time showed Henry VIII and Thomas Cromwell how to deal with them to the king's advantage, Wolsey never came to York at all. When, in the last summer of his life and abandoned by Henry, he set out for his installation in the Minster, he was arrested at Cawood and died on the journey south again to face a charge of high treason. With a finger in every political pie in the land, he had, however, tried to help the ailing economy of the city, and the dean of the cathedral during his tenure of the see had, unlike many of his predecessors and successors, at least resided in York and conscientiously attended chapter meetings.

In 1536 York witnessed and abetted the Pilgrimage of Grace, the only serious popular protest evoked by Henry VIII's proceedings against the church. Wolsey's successor as archbishop, the nervous Edward Lee, had presided over the historic meeting of the Northern Convocation in the chapter house on 5 May 1534. Here it was declared that the Bishop of Rome had no greater jurisdiction in the realm than any other foreign bishop. Lee preached on this proposition in the Minster and was instructed to persuade the north of its truth. Two years later, however, when the Pilgrimage passed through York, the Minster clergy met its leaders in procession in

Detail of early sixteenth-century glass, inserted in rose window of south transept as a gesture to or by the new dynasty: red Lancastrian roses alternate with white on red Tudor roses (deriving from Henry VII's marriage in 1486 with Edward IV of York's daughter)

Tomb of Archbishop Savage (d.1507) in north choir aisle; the last medieval monument in the Minster. The wooden chantry chapel above is a reconstruction of 1949

St William's College, founded 1461 for the Minster's chantry priests; much altered since its dissolution in 1547

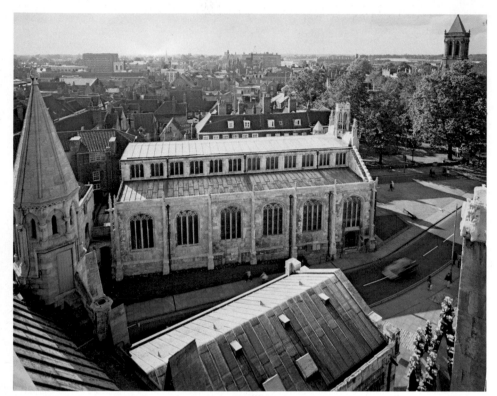

Church of St Michael-le-Belfrey rebuilt by the last medieval master-mason 1525–37, in the sparest late perpendicular style. The low building in the foreground is the old Minster library, built at an angle to the south transept c.1420

the cathedral; Lee himself, under duress, first joined and then disowned the revolt. The northern rebellion, put down by Henry VIII with a mixture of deception and brutality, was a protest against the new order in London, against the first dissolutions of abbeys and priories, against the dimly sensed end of a thousand years of a certain kind of piety. It was also the last spasm of the Wars of the Roses. Remnants of the house of York, minding their own business in the south, were mopped up for complicity with its aims; Scropes, Nevilles, Percys and Vavasours marched with the gentry and peasants who made it a real danger to the government. When Henry VIII made his only visit to York in 1541, the city fathers crawled in abasement before him, the new dean, Richard Layton, famous as a suppressor of monasteries, smashed St William's shrine as a gesture against popery, and in London the sixty-five-year-old Countess of Salisbury, daughter of Clarence and Isabel Neville and the last Yorkist in England, was executed on Tower Green.

Through all these decades of civil unrest, of bloodshed and treachery in high places, the life of the Minster continued. The residentiaries met in the chapter house and made their decisions. The great church, finished at last, teemed every day with people: priests, lawyers, choristers, pilgrims, penitents, pickpockets. Crowds of clergy scurried down its aisles and said masses at its many altars for long lists of the dead. The thirty-six vicars-choral, who performed the liturgical duties of the absent canons and lived in the college called the Bedern, had dwindled to about twenty in the sixteenth century, but chantries continued to be founded in the cathedral right up to Henry VIII's reign and the extra twenty or so priests needed to serve them were housed in St William's College, a Neville foundation of the 1460s. Nor were the Minster workshops idle: not only did the huge building have to be kept in repair, but in 1525 the last Gothic master-mason and his craftsmen embarked on the complete reconstruction of St Michael-le-Belfrey, the parish church immediately to the south of the cathedral. It was finished in 1537, after the Pilgrimage of Grace, and less than ten years before the government of Edward VI began the drastic dismantling of ancient observance in the Minster. By then York had a Protestant archbishop and the whole complicated fabric of medieval religious life was rapidly disappearing into the past.

CHAPTER 7

From the Reformation to the Present Day

Tomb of the Hon Augustus Duncombe, Dean of York 1858–80, south transept. Appointed because he was rich, he became one of the great deans of Victorian England and set the Minster on the course it has followed to the present day

It is ironic, and a reflection of the bewildering confusion of the times, that Robert Holgate, the first Protestant, and also married, Archbishop of York, was the only monk to hold the office since Henry Murdac. As Master of the Gilbertines, the one purely English monastic order, he had presided over the dissolution of the twenty-four houses in his care, and accepted a pension of £360 a year from Henry VIII (ordinary monks received pensions of between five and eight pounds). As Archbishop of York throughout Edward VI's reign, he saw the Minster stripped of half its clergy, all its chantries, altars, images, hangings and ancient vestments, and much of its plate and other treasure. He also handed over to the king sixty-seven manors, a large slice of the endowment of the see of York. Some of these depredations were, it is true, balanced by Protestant benefits: the remaining clergy were encouraged to improve their scriptural knowledge and their preaching; schools and almshouses were founded with the archbishop's personal wealth; texts from the Bible were inscribed in gold letters over the new communion table that replaced the high altar and its statues. The library lost all but one of its Saxon and Norman books and almost all of the cathedral's medieval charters, but gained important theological works that were now in favour. When Edward's Catholic sister Mary came to the throne, however, Holgate was deprived of the see for being married (and ignominiously shed his wife and his Protestant opinions to save his skin); the queen gave back most of the lost endowment; and the master-mason who had designed St Michael-le-Belfrey lived to restore what he could of the Minster's altars and furnishings.

Such reversals of the government's religious policy, each closely affecting the daily life of the Minster clergy and the internal appearance of the building, did not come to an end with the accession of Queen Elizabeth in 1558. Her settlement of the church

Below Part of ruined cloister; all that remains of the medieval archbishops' palace, north of the Minster, destroyed under Elizabeth I

was a compromise between the Catholicism-without-the-pope established as a state religion under Henry VIII and the fiery Protestantism of those martyred and exiled under Mary. It retained bishops (where most of the Reformed churches of Europe did not), and at the same time strongly enforced conformity to a moderate Protestant liturgy. This has remained ever since the basis of the Church of England, though it was a hundred years before the political upheavals surrounding its conception subsided sufficiently to allow it to settle down into a stable system. The problems raised by the attempt to uphold the compromise can be seen in the story of the late sixteenth and early seventeenth century Minster.

In 1559 Mary's archbishop, Heath, and half the chapter had resigned at the second withdrawl of allegiance to Rome. (The dean Nicholas Wotton remained in office from 1544 to 1567, his staying-power through the religious transformations of four reigns showing a personal ability to compromise of a very high, or low, order — particularly since he was Dean of Canterbury at the same time.) These old papist clerics were kindly treated by Elizabeth: no bigot herself, she had noted the counter-productive effects of her sister's persecution. But in York her archbishops set themselves to eliminate every remnant of the old ways from the Minster and the city. There was more physical destruction inside the Minster under Elizabeth than at any other period: to abolish the lingering belief in purgatory and prayer for the dead, so strong an element in pre-Reformation piety, tombs, brasses, coats of arms, portraits in the glass of windows, were removed along with altars, hangings and vestments. The memorials of many archbishops, deans and prebendaries, the clergy who had served the cathedral for three centuries and added their names to its fabric, disappeared.

Motives, as usual, were mixed. Archbishop Young pulled down the great hall of the archbishops' palace in order to sell the lead on the roof to his own profit. Archbishop Grindal, on the other hand, a convinced Calvinist and an exile under Mary like his successor Sandys, bombarded chapter and province with injunctions (sixty-nine of them) designed to root out every custom and object connected with Roman observance. By the 1570s an anti-papist campaign was in any case a political necessity in the north, since the Percys and Nevilles had been attempting to raise support for the Catholic Mary, Queen of Scots, and the might of Philip of Spain was beginning to threaten England. York recusants were forced to listen to Protestant sermons in the Minster; by 1600 thirty-four of them had died for their beliefs.

It came more easily to these Puritan archbishops to attack Catholicism than to defend the opposite flank of their Anglican middle-ground. The more extreme Puritans regarded the cathedral chapters and even the reformed episcopate as strongholds of idle privilege fit only for abolition. In the face of this growing ideological threat archbishops concentrated on the less controversial bullying of Catholics: Guy Fawkes, born in York and educated at the Minster's school, increased the national terror of Rome. Tobias Matthew, the most distinguished archbishop (1606–28) of the seventeenth century, did his best to clear the province of recusants. His Puritan widow left his splendid collection of three thousand books to the Minster to become the core of the present library. Both of them were horrified at the glamorous career of their son Sir Toby, poet, wit, friend of Bacon and Donne, and a Catholic convert who was ordained priest by St Robert Bellarmine.

It was possible however for Sir Toby Matthew to live to an unmolested old age, for in the reign of Charles I the religious pendulum swung again. The civilized French-inclined court and the high ritualism of Laud, the Archbishop of Canterbury, eased the pressure on Catholics though it inspired the righteous fury of the Puritans. The

Carved Jacobean monument, south choir aisle, to the Puritan Matthew Hutton, dean 1567–89, Archbishop 1596–1606; Elizabeth I's last Archbishop of York. He lies mitreless, in a Calvinist cap

Painted Jacobean monument, south choir aisle, to Edmund Bunney (d.1618), Calvinist theologian and canon of York; he kneels at the gate of heaven, surrounded by pious texts and scorning the terrestrial globe he has left behind

Prayer-book of Charles I, given by him to the Minster in 1633; keys of St Peter mounted at the corners; royal arms in the centre; rose of England and thistle of Scotland on the clasps

Laudian Neile, Archbishop of York from 1632 to 1640, reorganized the liturgical life of the Minster according to the new trend: gilding and bright colours, plate and altar-frontals returned, and 'a most excellent-large-plump-lusty-full-speaking organ', which cost a thousand pounds, brought music back to the cathedral. The king himself was impressed by the magnificence of the ceremonial when he visited the Minster in 1633, and he ordered the clutter of houses built against the south and west walls and the clutter of seats in the choir to be taken away to improve things still further. But the days of Charles I, as of the Laudian ideas which he so misguidedly attempted to impose on his Calvinist subjects in Scotland, were already numbered.

In 1639 York became again the effective capital of England. War with Scotland was expected and Charles set up his headquarters in the city. Although the final outbreak of civil war was delayed for three years, the alliance between the Scots and the parliament which Charles was compelled to call in 1641 put York at the strategic centre of the realm. In 1642 royalist pamphlets poured from the press set up in St William's College. Charles, harking back to ancient precedents, tried to summon parliament to York. Parliament would not come. By the spring of 1644 York was entirely surrounded by the soldiers of the king's enemies. The siege lasted three months. The royalist nobility and gentry of the county prayed for deliverance in the Minster. 'If York be lost', the king told Prince Rupert, 'I shall esteem my crown little else.' On 5 July Cromwell defeated the royalists at Marston Moor, seven miles away, and eleven days later the king's garrison marched out of the city in honourable defeat between the ranks of watching Roundheads. The drums beat and the colours flew for the last moment in history when the fate of the nation was decided at York.

The archbishop, John Williams, had fled to Wales in 1642; the dean was in prison for debt in London: after the surrender the parliamentarians held a victory service in the cathedral. Their commander Sir Thomas Fairfax, Cromwellian general and Yorkshire gentleman, allowed no damage to be done to the building, and the Minster thus escaped the wrecking inflicted on many cathedrals by fanatical Puritan icono-clasts.

Right Monument to Archbishop Dolben (d.1686), south choir aisle; a cavalier wounded at Marston Moor, faithful supporter of the monarchy and the Anglican church; contrast his mitred baroque confidence with the Puritan humility of his Jacobean predecessors

Monument to Archbishop Lamplugh (d.1691), a notorious changer of sides; by Grinling Gibbons, south choir aisle

It soon became clear that the Protestant city authorities were more in sympathy with the king's enemies than with his supporters. A Puritan committee, with Parliament's support, dissolved the chapter, without personal vindictiveness, and appointed four preaching ministers to inspire the religious life of the city from the Minster's pulpit. Away, again, went the organ, the altars, the hangings and the candlesticks; this time, however, the proceeds of sales went towards the upkeep of the fabric and there was no looting or profiteering. Archbishop Williams died in Wales in 1650; meanwhile the Commonwealth abolished episcopacy, and he was not replaced. For sixteen years the Minster belonged to the citizens as never before or since. Stripped of all the trappings of its Catholic and Laudian past, it echoed to Puritan sermons attended by aldermen and merchants relishing the absence of pomp and prelates. This was the pendulum's furthest swing to the left.

With the Restoration of Charles II in 1660, it came sharply back to the right (though not all the way to the Laudian extreme). Bishops were restored; deans and chapters were given back their revenues and their authority; the Book of Common Prayer, organ music, altars and Anglican ceremonial reappeared, this time for good. The new Archbishop of York, Accepted Frewen (1660–4), was born to a Puritan father in the year of the Armada, but was now rewarded for his fidelity to high-church principles and the king. The new dean, Richard Marsh, reappropriated all the old endowments and privileges of the Minster and separated it again from the influence — and also from the daily religious life — of the city.

Part of Lord Burlington's spendid neo-classical marble floor, covering the whole area of the Minster and involving the demolition of many medieval tombs; 1730–6

The institutional structure re-established at the Restoration survived intact until the 1840s. Much of it survives to this day. In form it goes back to the Norman Conquest and the arrangements made for the government of his cathedral by Archbishop Thomas of Bayeux. But the Minster of the late seventeenth century and after was not the Minster of the Middle Ages, nor of the Elizabethan settlement, nor even of Charles I's decorous vision. The long dislocation of the Reformation, with all its complex political and religious consequences, had broken continuities that could not be restored. By 1700 the attempt to impose religious uniformity on the nation had been abandoned; Catholic recusants on the one hand and Nonconformists on the other were persecuted no more; John Wesley, the strongest Christian force of the English eighteenth century, made his conversions and set up his Methodist Circuits outside the Anglican fold. With the dynastic troubles of the monarchy and the development of party politics, the Church of England become closely bound up with the Stuart cause, with the Tory party, with the network of patronage and influence by

Monument to Sir George Savile (d.1784), radical Whig M.P. for Yorkshire 1759–83, holding the 1780 Freeholders' Petition; north choir aisle. This statue of a provincial Voltaire, complete with Athenian owl, was erected in 1789, an embarrassing year for radicals

Truncheons of York Minster Police: cathedral law-enforcement in the Liberty of St Peter survived into the nineteenth century; the Minster prison was visited by the reformer John Howard in the late eighteenth century and still held one inmate in 1832

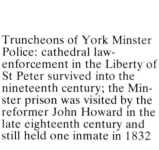

which Georgian England was governed. York became detached from national history, archbishops from independent secular power, the Minster from the mundane preoccupations of the city and the northern province. Regular services, of course, continued to be held in the choir. But in the sleepy, venal, theologically torpid religious atmosphere of the eighteenth century, the sense of their intrinsic value, whether people attended them or not, was weaker than ever before or since. Amidst the fragmentation of all that had made it possible for a county town at the edge of Christendom to construct one of the great churches of the world, the story of the Minster necessarily contracts to the story of a building and its maintenance by those in charge of it. The archbishops whose baroque and Victorian monuments somewhat incongruously adorn the choir aisles played much less part in this story than the deans in whose hands responsibility for the fabric actually lay.

Eighteenth-century taste, confident in its neo-classical judgement, regarded the accretions of the Gothic centuries with scant respect. The Palladian architect Lord Burlington designed a new floor for the whole Minster in 1730. This black and white key-patterned marble expanse, a foot higher than its predecessor, took six years to lay, and involved the destruction of every remaining tomb in the nave and many others in the transepts and choir. It is a handsome floor; it is also the last major piece of work in the Minster to have been undertaken wholly in the spirit of its own age. The guiding impulse hereafter was to be antiquarian, the object of almost all work and expenditure invisible restoration.

Throughout the period from the Restoration to the 1820s deans were faced with recurring damage to the building caused by gales, lightning and fires. Running repairs, especially to the roofs and windows, were also often necessary, and not always carried out. The deans did their best, with little support from the public. In 1770 subscription lists were opened by Dean Fountayne to raise the £4,000 needed

Sunflower at centre of rose window, south transept, by the York glass-painter William Peckitt; mid-eighteenth century

for immediate repairs. By 1788 only £697 15s had come in, and two hundred guineas of that had been given by the archbishop. Poor Dean Fountayne, who held the office for over half a century (1747–1801), was not greatly admired. In 1765 he replaced the Minster's bells; 'the inhabitants of York', wrote one of them, 'thought they had no reason to thank the Dean for meddling . . . for the old bells were much better, as well as the former dean.' Fountayne, at the end of the century, authorized the much-needed cleaning of the Minster's interior: this operation unfortunately included the obliteration of all the surviving medieval gilding and painting with a thick lime and ochre wash. It was also under Fountayne's direction that the York glass-painter William Peckitt devoted forty years of his life to the restoration and amendment of the Minster's windows, conscientiously, if sometimes clumsily, done, with a deferential eye to the unrepeatable splendour of the medieval glass.

Dean Markham (1802–22) inaugurated the first major restoration to the outside of the cathedral. The last extraneous buildings, including a watch-turret on the central tower, were cleared away; the west front was repaired and its most battered statues replaced; and the long-disused chapel of the old archbishop's palace was made into a new library. All these undertakings were in the normal line of decanal duty, given the continuing existence of the Minster as a functioning metropolitan cathedral which must not be allowed to decay. But Markham's successor, the talented, tactless, sadly isolated Dean Cockburn (1822–58) found himself confronted by the most serious crisis in the whole of the Minster's history.

In 1829 a disastrous fire started by a madman destroyed all the roof of the eastern arm, the choir stalls and the organ. Subscriptions towards the hugely expensive restoration were generous but did not meet the whole cost. In 1840 a second, accidental, fire burned down the nave roof and left the nave, the south-west tower and the south aisle as shells. This time the public response to the appeal for money was less generous and by the 1850s the Minster was deep into debt, the glass and stonework were decaying, and a survey of 1842 had revealed weaknesses in the piers of the central tower which there were no funds to remedy. What was more, the resources of the cathedral were being depleted by the slow effects of the 1840 Act of Parliament which deflected ancient chapter endowments to new industrial parishes,

Victorian Gothic memorial, 1862, south choir aisle, to two canons of York, William Mason (d.1797) and his nephew W. H. Dixon (d.1854); strikingly un-medieval for all its good intentions

and the dean's financial indiscretions had resulted in a shocking public dispute with the archbishop, In all the centuries of the life of the Minster, both as building and as institution, this was the moment when its fortunes reached their lowest ebb. Liturgical observance was in decline: the music was in a poor state, and the dean had for a time stopped the celebration of even weekly Communion. In fairness to Cockburn it must be said that this decline had been a long one. In 1756 Laurence Sterne had preached on All Saints' Day to 'one bellowsblower, three singing men, one vicar and one residentiary', and the early Evangelical, William Richardson, succentor in the late eighteenth century, had been the only Minster preacher of renown since the days of the Commonwealth.

To a Minster reduced to this dismal condition the prime minister, Lord Derby, in 1858 appointed as dean an aristocratic clerical younger son called Augustus Duncombe, with no apparent qualifications for the post except his wealth. Dean Duncombe, tactful, generous, tireless and always about, rescued the cathedral from financial chaos and resumed the architectural improvements, clearing old tenements which had obscured both east and west fronts, as well as restoring the south transept, the only part of the building undamaged in either great fire. He also, and more importantly, reorganised the religious life of the Minster. Inspired by the high-church idealism of his Oxford youth, he gave conviction, purpose and beauty back to the cathedral's liturgical routine. He lit and heated the nave so that it could be used for large services and musical events; he improved the morale and quality of the choristers and organist; he started the regular celebration of the sung Eucharist, making York the first cathedral to hold such services since the Reformation. At his death in 1880 the Minster's worship was set in the pattern which his successors have followed with only minor variations for a century.

They have followed him also, of course, in their unceasing care for a building which becomes always frailer, always more vulnerable to decay, corrosion, vibration, collapse, as the costs of maintenance and restoration rise and the real value of the cathedral's own resources fall. The story of the Minster in the hundred years since 1880 is the story of the struggle to preserve a noble artefact which is also an anachronism in an age when ecclesiastical Christianity plays a significant part in the lives of only a minority. The ups and downs of the story tell us as much about the times we live in as about the great structure of stone, lead, timber and glass which is at its centre.

For decades there has not been enough money, for ordinary running expenses, for heating the building in winter, above all for the constant repair and replacement of crumbling stonework. In spite of the ever-increasing number of sightseers, now about two million every year, who visit the Minster, there is still not enough money. On the other hand, specific projects and crises have found public support, for particular reasons. The surge of emotion evoked by the First World War produced generous donations for regimental chapels and other memorials to the war dead, including the Five Sisters window, restored in 1923–5 with lead which had been buried at Rievaulx Abbey since its dissolution in 1538. But appeals for the fabric as a whole, and for the restoration of all the glass, were met with apathy in the 1920s and 30s. In the period between the end of the Second World War, when the glass had been taken out for safe-keeping, and his death in 1963, Dean Milner-White was able to organize a heroic undertaking: the restoration of all the medieval windows, the sorting out of a vast jigsaw puzzle which the confused efforts of centuries had created.

The rescue of the endangered Minster took five years (1967–72) and cost £2 million: concrete collars and steel rods support the central piers below the present floor; beside them, rough medieval masonry and red-lined plaster facing of the exterior wall of 1080

The west front under restoration in July 1971
(Photo: Shepherd Building Group Ltd.)

But this, and the eventual setting up of the York Glaziers Trust, was largely financed by the Pilgrim Trust, an outside charitable foundation.

Then, in 1967, a two-year survey of the building by the new Minster architect, Bernard Fielden, revealed a structural crisis of horrifying proportions. His report showed the cathedral to be in actual danger of collapse: within fifteen years it would be unable to withstand the repairs necessary to save it. The response to the appeal for money, particularly in Yorkshire, was prompt, warm and sufficient. Two million pounds paid for the most drastic scheme to preserve a medieval building ever put into operation. The piers of the central tower were strengthened with collars of concrete

Concrete and steel underpinning of the central tower with the fifteenth-century choir screen above, 16 June 1971
(Photo: Shepherd Building Group Ltd.)

tied to the failing Norman foundations by twenty thousand feet of steel rods. The central tower was braced, high above the ground, by more steel rods, re-roofed, and its vault restored. Both the leaning east front and the west front had their foundations massively strengthened, and the western towers were stiffened against decay and the weather by further steel girdling and by the pumping in of thousands of gallons of liquid concrete. In 1972 the Minster, in an unprecedented blaze of publicity, celebrated the completion of the rescue work, a triumph of collaborative skill, at the five hundredth anniversary of the original completion of the building. Down in the undercroft (the excavated space beneath the floor of the central tower), the juxtapositions of Roman, Saxon, Norman, Gothic and brand-new masonry give the visitor a dizzying glimpse into that fourth dimension, time, the passing centuries, in which the architect, engineers and craftsmen had to work. Among much else, the rescue was a stunningly successful archaeological dig, clarifying for the present and the future the earliest history of the site, the church and the city.

Restoration never ceases: roof boss of south transept vault, removed 1979, riddled with death-watch beetle

New roof boss, inserted in south transept vault 1979

Paint and gold leaf applied, high in the vault, by one of the Minster's permanent staff of craftsmen; south transept 1979

Why did people respond in the way they did when the ultimate disaster threatened the Minster? Why should they continue to support the dean and chapter's long and expensive programme of repairs and maintenance, thirty years' work at least for the masons, wood-carvers and glaziers employed full-time by the cathedral? Because the Minster is beautiful, because it is unique; because it is the mother-church of northern England; because it is very old, grand and large. But perhaps the Minster is loved — and that is what the two million pounds meant, and what, in their way, the two million visitors each year also mean — most of all because it is a shared form, a communal expression of meaning and value which is available to everyone from the simplest to the most sophisticated. There was a time in our history when this was true of Christianity, when the glory of God was universally understood and received in a certain way, in certain words, under certain forms. It is no longer so; but the Minster, like the other great cathedrals, survives, a whole amongst the fragments of that time, still holding that common aspiration in its stone, belonging to no one, belonging to us all. During the fire of 1840, when the nave roof collapsed, 'a sudden glare of fire lit up the smoke and darkness within; the great crucifix in the west window of the south aisle shone out distinct and beautiful, and the cordon of soldiers, which surrounded the building to keep back the crowds, involuntarily raised their right hands and saluted.'

South transept full of scaffolding for the restoration of the roof, 1979; Five Sisters windows just visible in the north transept beyond

Plan of the Minster

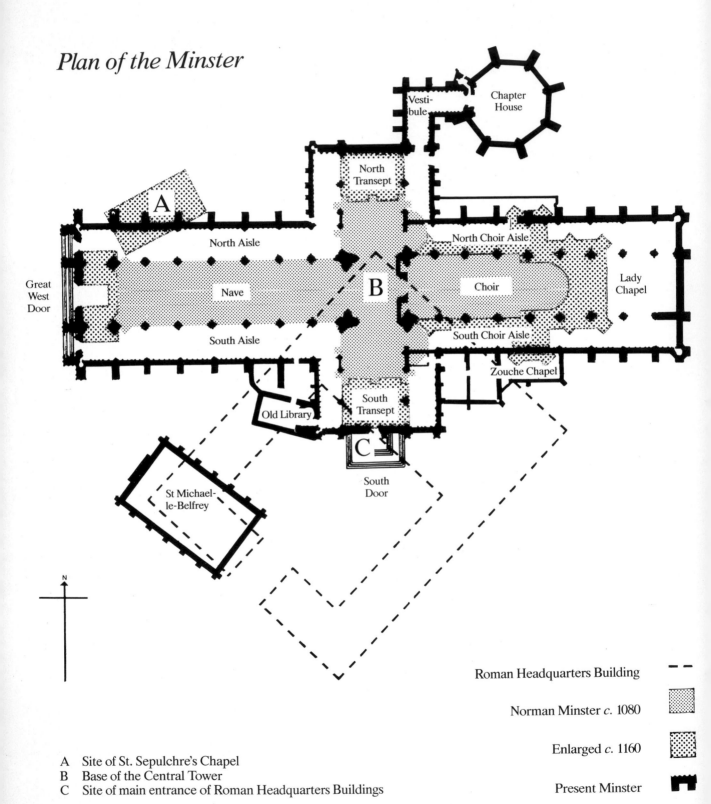

Chapter House

Vesti-bule

North Transept

A

North Aisle

North Choir Aisle

Great West Door

Nave

B

Choir

Lady Chapel

South Aisle

South Choir Aisle

Old Library

South Transept

Zouche Chapel

C

St Michael-le-Belfrey

South Door

N

Roman Headquarters Building

Norman Minster *c.* 1080

Enlarged *c.* 1160

Present Minster

A   Site of St. Sepulchre's Chapel
B   Base of the Central Tower
C   Site of main entrance of Roman Headquarters Buildings

Minster Information

The Minster is open to visitors every day of the week, from 7.00 am until after Evensong in winter, and until up to 8.30 pm during the peak summer season, but no sightseeing is permitted before 12.30 pm on Sundays, because of services.

Like any other church, York Minster is primarily a place of worship. There are prayers in the choir at midday for all who would like to join in, and throughout the tourist season there is a priest normally available in the building for consultation by visitors. The Zouche Chapel, off the south choir aisle, is reserved at all times for individual prayer and meditation, and sightseers are asked to respect the privacy of those using it for this purpose. For those who would like to attend one of the regular services that are held daily in the Minster, the following is a list of times that do not normally vary throughout the year.

Weekdays: Matins every day at 7.40 am
Holy Communion every day at 8.00 am
                  on Wednesdays also at 11.30 am
                  on Fridays also at 12.30 pm
Evensong (sung, except on Wednesdays) every day at 4.00 pm

Sundays: Holy Communion at 8.00 am
                  and at 8.45 am
Sung Eucharist at 10.15 am
Matins (sung) at 11.30 am
Evensong (sung) at 4.00 pm

Guided tours of the Minster are available from 9.30 am to 3.30 pm and from 5.00 pm to closing time on weekdays, and from 1.00 pm to 3.30 pm and 5.00 pm to closing time on Sundays. Visitors enquiring at the Information Desk in the south aisle of the nave during these hours will be put in touch with a guide (or a verger on Sundays) as soon as one is free. To avoid disappointment, however, and particularly in the case of parties or school trips, intending visitors are strongly advised to contact the Tourist and Information Office, giving as much advance notice as possible, at St William's College, College Street, York YO1 2JF — telephone (0904) 24426 — to whom all other enquiries in connection with visits to the Minster should also be addressed.

Access to the chapter house (entry in the north transept), to the central tower, and to the permanent exhibition in the undercroft and treasury (both in the south transept), is by payment. Access to the crypt and the shrine of St William is free, on application to one of the Minster guides or vergers.

In St William's College, opposite the east end of the Minster, there is a Brass Rubbing Centre (open from 10.00 am on weekdays and 12.30 pm on Sundays, to 5.00 pm in winter and 6.00 pm in summer), and a self-service restaurant, open from 10.00 am to 5.00 pm, Mondays to Saturdays (party bookings on application to the manager — telephone 0904 34830).

The Minster from the north